OTHER TITLES BY THAD KRASNESKY

From Flashlight Press

I Always, Always Get My Way

That Cat Can't Stay

Pterodactyl Show and Tell

From Schiffer Publishing

Fright to the Point

The Cat from Kabul

THAD KRASNESKY

Cover art designed by Isabelle Krasnesky

ISBN # 979-8-218-19266-2

Cat Manor Press

This book is, of course, dedicated to No Tail.
He and I were the lucky ones.

Contents

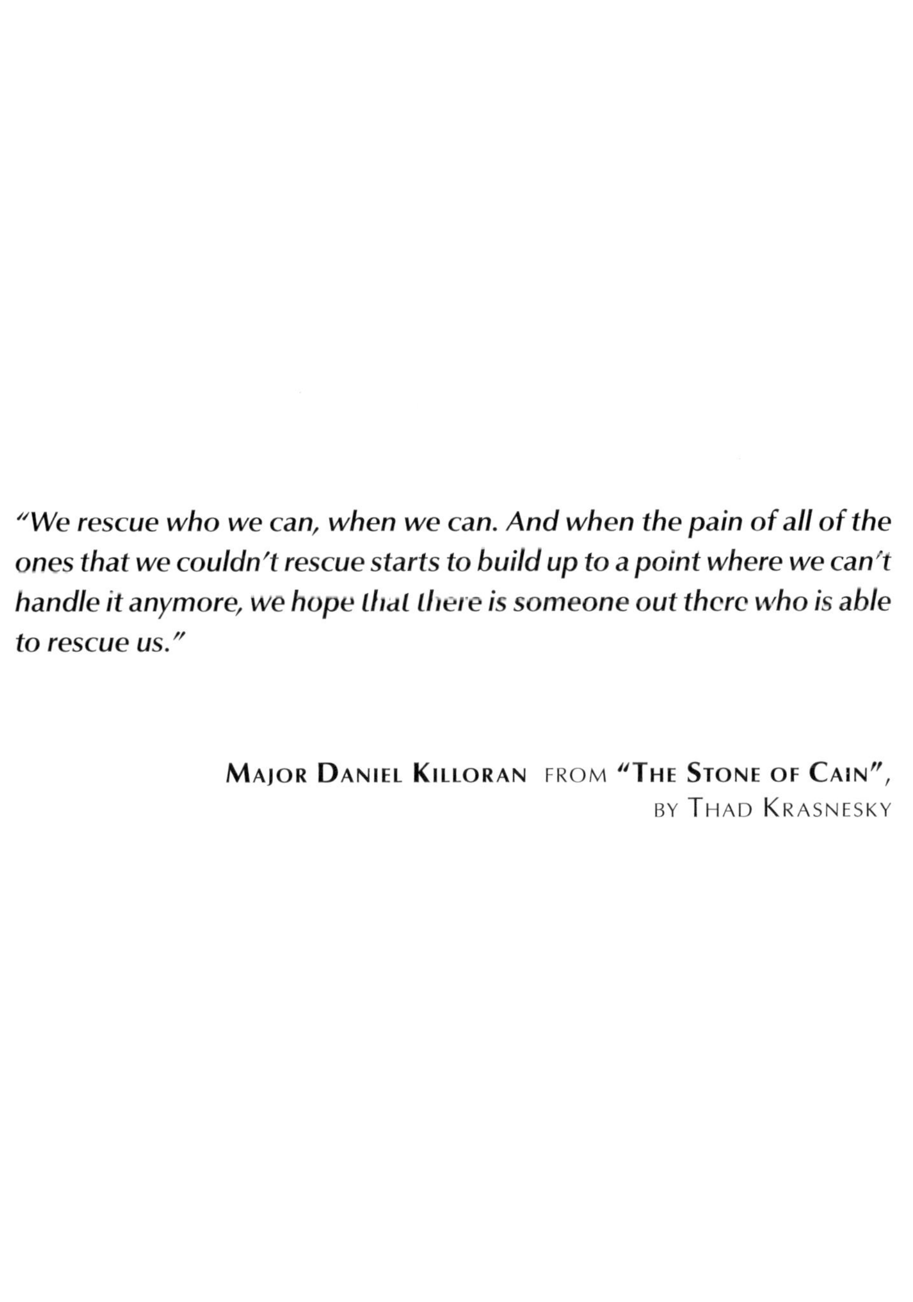

"We rescue who we can, when we can. And when the pain of all of the ones that we couldn't rescue starts to build up to a point where we can't handle it anymore, we hope that there is someone out there who is able to rescue us."

Major Daniel Killoran from **"The Stone of Cain"**,
by Thad Krasnesky

Foreword

This book was written by an unsupervised author. That is never a good idea. There is a reason we need editors, and if you are an editor reading this, my apologies for the multiple heart attacks you are about to have. There will be misspellings. There will be typos. There will be grammatical errors. Lots of them. Conceptually, I know that commas are a thing, but the practical application of them is often subject to my attention span and a sense of literary whimsy.

There will be sidebars that may not get back to the original point for several pages. There will be dead-ends where I wander off down one path and get lost. There will be sections that look like unsuccessful cut-and-paste jobs from chapters that got deleted, because they probably are. And there will be sentences that start with "and" and run on for way too long because I tend to write as I speak, especially when it is something that I am worked up about, which is most of this book, so it might help if you read this book as if it were me speaking to you.

That is really what this book is. Just a conversation between friends. Me and you. Sitting down so that I can tell you about someone that is important to both of us.

I am going to be talking for a while so let me grab a glass of water and then we can get started.

No Tail Before Me

The dust continued to rise into his mouth, insisting on being eaten. He could not afford to expend the effort or the moisture necessary to spit it out, so he swallowed it down and kept running. Besides, he had not eaten breakfast that day, and the sweat turned the irritating, yellow dust into a salty, mud porridge in his mouth, which he supposed was better than nothing.

From, **"The Menorah of Vespasian"**, by Thad Krasnesky

Bibi Mahru
RS
تعلیمات، کمک، مشورت

I

There is a road in Kabul called the Bibi Mahru. It runs roughly north and south and connects the international airport to the administrative center of the city. It is a loud and dusty thoroughfare, that cuts through the loud and dusty bowl of the city that is Kabul.

Traffic along the Bibi Mahru is constant, but not as heavy as it is along other major roads in the city. The many government buildings that line both sides of the street for a two mile stretch through the center of the city have generated a requirement for a series of roadblocks and gates to ensure security. These obstacles have encouraged many drivers to choose alternate routes, such as the Shash Darak to the east or the Wazir Khan to the west.

The automobile though is a conveyance of convenience, and thousands of drivers still race up and down the Bibi Mahru every day, slamming on the brakes at one gate only to stomp on the gas as soon as the gate is raised, rushing from one check point to the next, choosing the shortest route over the least obstructed route. Cab drivers are cab drivers, whether you are in New York or Kabul, and time is money.

Near the southern end of the Bibi Mahru, just north of the Spanish Embassy, is a small park that covers about a fourth of a city block. During the week, the park is home to a few vendors that have permanent booths set up under the dusty, twisted mesquite trees. During the weekend however, the park fills to overflowing with hundreds of vendors that set up tables, or carpets, or boxes anywhere they can find space. They shove into every unoccupied nook of the marginally green park, with the unluckiest and least aggressive vendors being pushed into the embraces of the lackluster shrubs and Jerusalem thorn bushes that grow along the parks abandoned edges.

This struggle for space causes the weekend markets to spill across the Bibi Mahru onto a thin strip of empty ground on the east side of the road. When that small overflow space fills up, the haphazard vendors drip even further away from the central traffic artery, down a long alley, until the unluckiest or least aggressive of them finally pool together in an endorheic dead end that is wedged between a soccer pitch on one side, and a security wall on the other.

It was somewhere within this narrow, vendor-filled alley, in 2008, that a small, black kitten was born. He would likely have been one of a litter of maybe four or five brothers and sisters. The vendors in the bazaar would likely have been too focused on fighting for their space, and selling their goods, and not getting stuck by thorns to notice the kitten or his litter mates, tucked under some bush or secreted in some pile of rubble. The motorists on the nearby Bibi Mahru were too intent on maneuvering through the series of checkpoints on their way to wherever they were going to even notice the vendors, much less the new, mewing arrivals.

Beyond the Bibi Mahru, the four million residents of the capital city of Afghanistan were doing what most people do best; focusing on themselves and simply trying to survive, and beyond Kabul, less and less attention was being paid to the city, or even the country, which had once been integral to the semi-mythical Silk Road, and had a history as glorious as it was bloody.

Somewhere there were people reading stories about Afghanistan or planners developing military contingencies for Afghanistan, but they were only engaging with and thinking about Afghanistan as a concept. They were not spending time thinking about the reality of it all, or the residents of the city, or of the motorists on the Bibi Mahru, or the vendors in the park, and it is a certainty that no one in the entirety of the world was sparing a thought at that moment for the small black kitten that had just been born, and had just begun his own fight for survival.

II

Feral kittens stay with their mothers until they are between eight and twelve weeks old. By that point in their development, they have learned to hunt for themselves and are expected to move away from their mother. Eight to twelve weeks. It is such an incredibly short period of time to be loved.

I don't know how many litter mates that No Tail had, and I don't know how old he was when he finally moved out on his own, but I hope that it was at least closer to the twelve-week timeline than the eight-week option. I know much of the life that he was about to live, and the struggles that he would endure, and I know that it would be many years before love played a part in his life again, so I hope his mother kept him for the entirety of those twelve weeks.

Kabul is a dusty place, and the market was dustier still, but I hope that his mother groomed him, and licked the dust from his fur, and kept him clean. The nights in Kabul can be cold, even during the summer, but I hope that she held him close and kept him warm. Kabul can also be a place of sudden and unexpected danger, but I hope that, for at least those first few weeks, she kept him safe.

I think about No Tail always. I often think about him as a kitten, and by extension, I will occasionally find myself thinking about his mother. I constantly wish that I had come across No Tail when he was still little, and saved him from the difficult life he was about to undergo, but almost as often as I wish that I could have spared him from the trauma that he would eventually endure, I often find myself wishing that I had some way of communicating with that mother cat, in the dusty market in Kabul, in 2008, and letting her know that someday I would find her little boy, and take care of him, and that everything would be alright in the end.

At the very least though, I can thank her here for whatever it was that she did for him, and whatever lessons there were that she imparted to him. Her efforts were not in vain.

Whatever the age he was when he got that last bath from his mother, when No Tail did finally leave the market area, there would have been four options available to him. He could have attempted to scale the security wall to the north. That would have led into the United Nations zone, and the area around the United States embassy. There was green grass there, and fountains, and people, and might have offered him the opportunity to bond with one of the state department employees who might have cared for him.

For a stray cat, it would not have been a bad life. There were already many cats that made their home on the large campus-like area. There was, however, the issue of the security wall. Beyond the security wall was a defensive perimeter, and then beyond that, chain-link fence, and barbed wire. It was not something that would be beyond his skills as an adult cat, but at twelve weeks old, it would have been a daunting obstacle.

He could have chosen to leave the market area and head into the greater Kabul world. The city sprawls for miles around, and he would likely have had a life not too different from the strays that wander the streets of any major city.

He could also have simply chosen to remain in the market. There were plenty of food vendors in the market, which meant that there would always be scraps for him to steal. There would also be plenty of mice and rats feeding on the refuse as well, which would have provided him with a constant food source to hunt.

Then there was the fourth option. Probably the worst option for a cat at that place and time. The fourth option was to head into the adjacent miliary base.

III

The Resolute Support base was a densely packed multi-national base next to the US Embassy. Service members from more than thirty nations worked and lived together on the base. Everyone shared one dining facility and one fitness center, but most nations had their own designated area of operations, where they conducted administrative functions, intelligence gathering, and vehicle maintenance. Flags might be different from one compound to the next, but the functions and the buildings within each were relatively similar.

The biggest difference between the many national compounds were the residential areas. Most permanent servicemembers and contractors resided in one of the four large dormitories on the base. They were new, multi-storied construction with two-person rooms, and communal bathrooms for every twenty or thirty rooms. They were clean, and only a small step down from what you might find on a modern college campus.

The Danish and Swedish troops, however, stood head and shoulders above the rest when it came to living spaces. They had modular living quarters that looked like something out of the military section of an Ikea catalog. Two to four service members would share a two-story Lego apartment that had all the amenities. A small but comfortable living room, clean and efficient bathrooms that were shared with five or six people instead of thirty or forty, and even a compact kitchen area where they could prepare their own food.

As far above the normal accommodations as the Scandinavian facilities were, there was a living area that was far beneath them as well. Situated at the opposite end of the residential spectrum, both in terms of comfort as well as in geography, were the grimy trailers that were shoved to the far end of the compound. The stacked sleeping spaces crammed into the sagging vinyl rooms required that at least one person would get stepped on when it came time to go to bed. The floors were bowed, and the walls and ceilings were too tired to do anything as dramatic as creaking, but they did sigh a lot. A few rooms were vacant, unacceptable even to deployed military sensitivities, due to deterioration, and the floors of the bathrooms were spongy, sinking in to an alarming degree when dozens of people would try and elbow their way into the tight spaces every morning to get an inch of counter space, or to queue up for their shot at thirty seconds or more of hot water from an unmotivated shower.

There was, of course, one level of living space that was even lower than the "let's pretend they don't exist" slumlord military trailers. That was the living condition for the stray cats on the post.

There had been both cats and dogs on the base at one time, but the military had decided that war against the Taliban did not provide enough opportunities for them to kill things, so they had also declared war against the strays on the base as well and had issued an order that all animals on the base were to be killed. This was very common at that time and was endemic to both theaters of war. It was an order that had been issued in Iraq as well when I had been stationed there in 2003-2004, and one that I had ordered my team to ignore. A few dogs had been shot by people who were with other units before I had let it be known that if a dog was identified as part of a terrorist group and was armed with an AK 47, and was actively shooting at you then it was okay to shoot back, but unless an animal presented an immediate threat to them, I would communicate to them strongly, in a non-verbal manner, what I thought of cowards who killed animals for the fun of it. I had already begun to manifest anger issues, even back then, but more about that later.

There is an actual need for animal control on military bases, as there is in any urban environment, but most people do not think through the process or consider the second and third order effects, so "kill them all" is the simplest solution. This quickly created the desired effect regarding the dogs. Dogs are generally larger than cats. They are usually not as adept at hiding. And even stray dogs are generally more friendly and interested in human companionship than cats are. The combination of these factors meant that it did not take long for the dog population to be eradicated.

The cats, however, endured. The attempt was made to wipe them out, but waging war on cats is as effective as waging war on anything that is conceptual and intangible.

This was why the living situation for the cats was even worse than sleeping on moldy aluminum that smelled like it might have digested its previous tenant. No living condition is as uncomfortable as knowing that you can be killed out of hand at any moment. This was the environment that three-month-old No Tail wandered into when he left the market. For the first year of his life, he would have struggled with natural predators, other cats, and the environment itself. He would have had to find food, and places to stay warm and dry. And in addition to all these challenges, he would also have had to evade the animal death squads.

I have had people try to kill me before. I know what it is like to be in mortal danger, but I have never had to accept that as part of my constant way of life. It is difficult to know how such things might change you unless you have experienced them firsthand. It is impossible to know how this environment contributed to forming the personality that would become the cat I came to love, but it is impossible for that type of environment not to have had some impact.

Fortunately for No Tail and the rest of the cats, and fortunately for the people on the base as well, the extermination order was rescinded in 2009. A veterinary support officer and their team were assigned to the base, and they were able to bring a degree of expertise to the situation that had previously been lacking. The officer would have likely been a relatively low-ranking officer, probably a lieutenant but no more than a captain at best. Somehow, they mustered the courage and the charisma to convince the senior officers on the base that the procedure that was currently in place was not the most effective means to the desired end. I don't know who it was. If anyone knows who that group was, or if it happens to be you, please call me. I owe you my life.

Instead of the extermination policy, this officer and their team instituted a monitoring and tracking policy, and eventually a fully developed TNR program was put in place. For those that do not know, TNR stands for "Trap, Neuter, and Release". The intention is to reduce the stray population through sterilization programs instead of extermination.

Two, large shipping containers were connected to create a long and narrow veterinary facility. A tracking board was placed in the veterinary support facility alongside a large, laminated map of the base. They began to record observations of cats on the base, and eventually they were able to plot the territory of each animal on the map. These reports were compiled by direct observation of the veterinary support staff, but also by speaking to people who had been stationed on the base.

It was late 2009 when a young, black, male cat was added to the board.

IV

The first unofficial report we have of No Tail came toward the end of 2008. People assigned to the intelligence facility on the base said that a young, black cat began showing up and watching people from a distance. This was still during the time of the great dog and cat eradication, and not only did the regulation state that stray animals were supposed to be killed, but it also clearly outlined that no personnel were under any circumstances to socialize with or befriend stray animals, and absolutely under penalty of extreme frowny faces from people with big rank on their collar were you supposed to ever provide food or water to these animals.

The personnel at the intelligence center, following the proud tradition of soldier's everywhere when faced with ridiculous orders from people who often don't know how to handle weapons properly but are certain that "being happy" somehow interferes with your ability to shoot, promptly set out a food and water bowl underneath a sheltered bench for the little kitten that they began to call Bear. For the first year of his life, until the kill order was rescinded, Bear was a communal secret. Outsiders that spotted the feeding station and asked about it were met with a response of, "What feeding dish?", because most of the time we can get away with stuff like that, but also because we probably watch too many sci-fi movies and most of us think we're Jedis.

Bear entered the official records a year later, when the veterinary support facility opened up. At first, it was just the verbal reports and visual confirmation. Black, male cat. That was the extent of it. A few months later, when he was trapped in one of the facility's live traps for the first time, a folder was started for him. Its information was sparse.

Male. Non-neutered. Multiple previous wounds. FIV positive, but otherwise generally healthy. Under two years old.

That was the extent of it. Nothing about what his favorite foods were or where he liked to be petted. No mention of how steady his purr was, or how his eyes would open wide when he became impatient and started howling. No remarking on how incredibly athletic he was and how his leaps seemed more like levitating than jumping. Not even a name.

He was neutered, and chipped, and given a tracking number, and then released back onto the base. The primary purpose for neutering TNR cats is to ensure that they do not reproduce, but the secondary goal is to make the cat less aggressive, which will generally lead to a healthier cat population, with fewer injuries from fighting. This procedure would not have the desired behavioral effect for Bear. Over the next three years, he would be trapped in one of the live traps three times, and each time he was examined, he was reported to have sustained even more severe injuries than the last time.

It is impossible to know if there was something in him that drove him to seek out fights, or if there was something about him that drew the fights to him. I knew him for nine years, and I have known myself for about the same length of time, and I suspect it was a little bit of both. There comes a point in your life when something inside you breaks. Like an old wind-up toy whose key has been turned so many times that the mechanisms inside just rattle about loosely like rusted pieces of a worn-out soul.

Predators hear the rattle of the broken bits inside and think that you are an easy target. What they don't realize is that once someone has been broken, they often have no concerns about being damaged further. And as long as you don't mind being hurt, it is easy to hurt back. A bigger, stronger predator can approach you threateningly and say, "I will win, and I will eat you," and if you cared whether or not you were eaten, that threat might hold some weight, but when you have stopped caring you simply smile back at them and say, "The best parts of me were devoured long ago."

So the broken little cat that left his mother's care in 2008 became more and more broken over time. Two of the three injuries that were recorded during that time were considered life-threatening, but neither of them seemed to slow him down.

Then, in 2012, the entries ceased. The black cat known as Bear stopped showing up at his feeding station at the intelligence center. Month after month passed drearily by without a record of him being drawn into one of the live traps by the smell of tuna. 2012 turned into 2013.

The personnel at the intelligence center still held out hope. Their aloof little mascot was a survivor. He exuded a sense of enduring. He had been wounded before and survived, so they watched for their little black Bear, certain he would overcome whatever the latest misfortune that had befallen him. Like faithful Britons awaiting the return of the king, they believed, and they waited.

Two years later, the king returned, but oh, the battles he had seen.

V

In TNR programs, when a cat disappears, that usually only means one thing. It means that the cat is deceased. It is always possible that the animal in question has moved on, but cats are territorial creatures and once they are adults, they do not often change their environment willingly.

The food dish under the bench was eventually put away, and the board in the veterinary center was updated. The file at the center was still maintained, but the number was removed from the active cat list and the map was updated to indicate that there was one less cat prowling the areas around the residence halls and the intelligence center.

The worst was assumed, then gradually acceptance settled in, and after the next rotation of soldiers and civilians cycled through the base, the black cat that had often sought shelter and food was mostly forgotten. Other cats moved into the vacated space in the urban ecosystem, and life moved on, as much as life can in a combat environment whose primary purpose is focused on ending life.

Then, in the spring of 2014, a skinny, bedraggled remnant of a cat limped into the entrance court of the intelligence center. The first people who spotted him thought initially that the cat might have some disease and were inclined to put it down, but one of the women who had recently arrived was a contractor that claimed to recognize this cat.

"That's Bear," she declared with certainty, and a food and water dish were immediately procured and set out for the returning monarch.

Bear, however, had changed. Not only was he emaciated and missing patches of fur, and even more heavily scarred than he had ever been, but he had also become resistant to being touched. Where before he had been aloof and cautious, now he was angry and fearful. Retreating and hissing whenever someone approached him and running away if someone persisted in reaching out to him.

It took weeks before he was finally able to be lured into a live trap and brought to the treatment center. The microchip was scanned, and it was confirmed that this was Bear. Upon examination, it was determined that the front leg and the back leg on his right side had both been broken, with the front leg likely having been broken in multiple places. The back hip appeared to have an odd alignment and a noticeable bone spur, indicating that the hip might also have been severely damaged. There were similar irregularities noted on several ribs.

Fur was still struggling to grow back over several patches of bare skin that were crossed with ragged and puckered scars. This was also the first time that a missing tail was noted on his file. The tail is one of the mysteries of No Tail that we will never be able to know for certain. It is possible that the lack of a tail was simply not recorded on earlier forms because some cats simply don't have tails, and if it was not the site of an injury then it is perfectly conceivable that a rushed administrative entry would have focused on the more relevant information. There are plenty of accounts from people on the base though that claim that No Tail once in fact had a tail, although eyewitness accounts are notoriously unreliable, and it is easy to believe that they are conflating one black cat with another.

It is my hope that the people who report having seen him with a tail as a younger cat are mistaken, because the veterinarian had two likely scenarios for how Bear came about his injuries. The first scenario is that he was struck by a vehicle. Broken legs and ribs and torn flesh are consistent with a collision with a car or a Humvee. The second option is that he was the victim of a deliberate attack by a person or persons. The injuries received would have also been consistent with being beaten.

Appendages like tails can become necrotic and simply fall off of an injured animal if it is not treated, so it is possible that losing a tail could have been the result of an accident, but if it was a deliberate attack then it is possible that cutting off his tail might have been part of the torture that he was subjected to. Neither one of these options are desirable, but I hope that he was born without a tail because if he had originally had a tail then it makes the second scenario slightly more likely, and that is something that my heart struggles to comprehend.

Whatever the cause, whether it was an accident or an attack or even the very unlikely but environmentally plausible option that he was caught in an IED explosion, the end result was devastating. The veterinarian was adamant that he could not have survived his injuries. It wasn't his opinion that it was unlikely. In his experience, it was simply not possible.

Somehow though, Bear had achieved the impossible. Infection would certainly have overwhelmed his system, but somehow, he fought it off and survived. Loss of blood should have ended him. Predators should have finished off the wounded animal, but they did not. Starvation and thirst should have definitely ended his life but somehow, he managed to not only move, but to move well enough to keep himself sustained.

I don't like to think of him hurting like that. I don't like to think of him lying in some ditch or hiding under some debris while he was racked with fever and pain and hunger, while rats and dogs circled him looking for an easy meal. I don't like to think of how much it must have hurt for him to drag himself to some dirty pool of water to slake his thirst, or how he would have swallowed any piece of grass or scrap of digestible food he could find to get something in his belly. I don't like to think about it, but I do. I think about it because I love him and I want to understand him and know him better, and in order to do that, I need to comprehend how much he went through.

More importantly though, I think about it because sometimes I need to remind myself what is possible. The will that it must have taken to not just simply give up and quit. To endure pain that defies any scale that we could possibly assign to it and keep going. I think about what he went through because he is what I strive to be. When I hurt and I'm tired and it feels like too much to keep going on, and like taking even one more breath is just no longer possible, I think of him and I redefine what the word possible means, and I take that next breath. It reminds me that I cannot let what he endured to have been endured in vain. Suffering rarely has a purpose. It isn't noble. But if I can find some way to create a positive change out of suffering then at least it won't have been for nothing.

The veterinarian debated at the time whether or not he should release the cat back onto the base or if it might be a better idea to take the cat to Now Zad, an animal rescue organization started in Afghanistan by a former British Special Forces soldier. The concern was that the cat would not be able to fend for itself and placing it with an organization where it might eventually become adopted would ensure a more positive outcome. After a few days in the clinic though, it was clear that this cat would never be anything but an angry feral. There was a brief consideration as to whether or not it would be kinder to euthanize him, but that option was quickly dismissed, and he was once more released back onto the base that he had called home for most of his adult life.

For the first few years of his life, he had been known by many as Bear, and had been recorded as a number at the veterinary facility. For almost two years, he had simply been gone. Now, after returning, with few still around that knew him as Bear, he was at first just referred to as "that cat without a tail". That was soon shortened and morphed into a new name.

No Tail.

VI

No Tail was a decidedly different personality when he returned than he had been previously. Wild cats are instinctively cautious. Ferals possibly even more so. They have the wild animal instinct, combined with a more integrated understanding of what a human is capable of.

Previously, No Tail had been cautiously approachable. If you were patient and acted in a non-threatening manner, you might be able to offer him snacks out of your hand, or even pet him. After the incident, however, he would not let anyone get close. He would come for the food that was set out for him, but if you even looked like you might be considering approaching him, he would sense it before you had even moved, and he would be off.

It is important to note though, that he continued to frequent the areas of human occupation. Although he wouldn't let you touch him, he was still drawn to seek out human companionship. He would sit just on the other side of the fence, watching people come and go to the facility, able to be seen but not able to be touched. He would lounge in the hedges and brush just off of the walkways or at the edge of the residential area, in full view of anyone passing by but never letting anyone get within a dozen feet of him. It was obvious that he knew how fast a person could move and how much distance they could cover in a single lunge, and he had no intention of ever existing within that sphere of possible entanglement.

Over time, a much more highly modulated version of his previous social interaction gradually began to return. Where before you could have slowly crept toward him, taking half a minute to cover a ten-foot distance, and he would have allowed you to approach him and even touch him, now those times and distances were magnified exponentially. If you went to the coffee kiosk on the base and saw him nearby, you could sit down on the ground thirty feet away and gradually use the next half an hour of your day to move a foot a minute and draw close.

Perhaps he felt compelled to reward people who were willing to invest that amount of time in him, but more likely it was that he recognized people with ill intent generally were the type that needed immediate gratification. Not that he would completely trust those who took their time. He was still aware that with enough motivation and malice, even those who intended evil could be patient, so even if you had invested the time to get close enough to pet him, any sudden movement could cause him to immediately bolt away, and then good luck in getting him to settle down for the next day or two.

It was this wounded, cautious version of No Tail that I would first meet in the spring of 2015.

Me Before No Tail

On Privilege

There are eight billion people on earth,

And it's such random chance that at birth

We end where we are now,

Yet still people somehow

Equate placement at nascence with worth.

"On Privilege", from **"Five Lines"**, by Thad Krasnesky

I

So, this is the part that I had to completely throw away and rewrite. One of my trial readers described the first version that I wrote as being too glib.

They weren't wrong. Which is a reluctant way of saying they were right. It was inauthentic, the way it was written initially. In hindsight I find it interesting how much easier it was for me to write about the violence and trauma I experienced later in life in relation to my childhood. I was pretty naked about those later truths. Blunt and unvarnished. Very direct.

The childhood part though was...

What was the phrase the reader used to describe it?

Oh yeah. A little too Jokey Smurf.

Psychologists will tell you, and by "psychologists" I mean my therapist, that humor is one of the more common masking techniques when people try to deal with trauma. If you want to see some people that have been through some stuff, find a good comedian. They're not performing when they are up there on stage. They are running. Masking the hell out of some shit.

Considering my background, there were really only two career choices that I was best suited for. Comedian or serial killer. So please excuse the bad jokes that I make as I write this. They are better than the other option, although if I am being honest, and not glib, that second career choice does make a few cameo appearances along the way.

I did work briefly as a comedian when I was in college. Worst performance I ever had was the night I convinced my parents to come to one of my sets. There wasn't even polite laughter that night. Not even from my parents. I think they would have laughed to show their support for me, but they didn't want the other people in the audience thinking they were stupid. It was that bad.

But I'm getting ahead of myself. I haven't even told you yet about how I was born in a hospital, and not beneath a thorny bush in a market in Afghanistan, thereby creating a contrasting but relatable narrative connection between my origin and No Tail's. Let's go back to the beginning of this section about me and see how authentic I can be this time. There is still going to be inappropriate humor, but I will try to make it less glib.

Honestly, if I were you, I would just skip this part. Start at part three, where I meet No Tail. This chapter is the most poorly written in the entire book and that's saying a lot, because there are some jumbled chapters awaiting you, but if I reread this part one more time, I may just decide to toss the whole thing. So you get what you get. Like I said in the foreword, it's just a conversation between friends, and sometimes friends ramble.

And if my trial reader thought the version they read was inauthentic, they should have seen the original version I wrote. The entire thing was in third-person, like I was writing a book report. Separation is another coping technique that people use to deal with trauma. The stories that we tell about trauma are often presented as if they happened to someone else.

Which is weird that I would have such an embarrassingly obvious trauma response to talking about my childhood, since as you will see, my childhood wasn't actually that traumatic. There were maybe a couple of incidents that I am still trying to figure out how to properly frame, so I can see how I might have gotten there, if I allowed myself to look at things a little more closely, which I don't think I'll do right now.

Mostly, I think the reason that speaking about childhood directly is more difficult is because it is more personal. More central to who we are. Childhood is where we develop into the self that has to deal with all of the other stuff that comes along, and since children tend to be more vulnerable than adults the things we experience in those soft, unformed moments in our lives are still more tender. It is why we can talk about killing someone as an adult more openly than we can talk about being thrown into the thorn bushes at the bus stop every morning in second grade.

See what I'm doing again? Writing things in the second person plural. Using "we" as if I'm talking to a class or addressing a group. Because unless "we" all had some odd, convergent childhoods, it's unlikely that "we" were all thrown into thorn bushes as a kid, and then went on to kill people later in life.

Damn. Even with a light application of casual, humorous bonhomie, that last line was harder to write than it should have been.

So anyway, I should probably stop writing about why I had to rewrite the opening section about my childhood and actually get on with writing it.

So...

Here we go.

Gonna just jump right in here.

On the count of three. One, two....

II

I was born in Chicago, but I was conceived in California. There is no real reason you need to know where I was conceived, but since I have to deal with the awareness of my parents having sex, I figure I might as well share it with you. It is also relevant because it speaks to the somewhat itinerant nature of our family in those first few years.

After a few years in Chicago, my parents moved to Arkansas when I was five. They wanted to "get away from it all." At five, what it felt to me like they were getting away from was my family, my house, my friends, my dog, and pretty much anything that a five-year-old would think of as civilization. I don't remember a lot from that time period. There was the car on fire in our driveway in Chicago, and then the next thing I knew, we were living in a tent in a field in Arkansas.

Ish. The next thing I knew-ish. There were a lot of other mixed-up sequences of memories in there. Bare feet on hardwood floors, cheesecake, a couple of brief stays in the hospital, snails in the dirt pile at the end of the street, candles at the church, and the last Christmas that I believed in Santa Claus when I was three. But I was five when we moved, so you can't expect me to keep all of those things straight in my head. Linearly, I remember the car on fire and then I remember the tent and eating beans out of a can cooked on a camp stove.

Poverty and a search for a place to call home was something that No Tail and I might have shared as we both began our lives, but one of the biggest differences, and a definite advantage that I had over No Tail in the beginning was that I had parents that were more long-term than twelve weeks. They had their struggles, as all parents do, but they stuck around.

My father taught me chess and gave me an ability to intuit consequences that were four and five levels deep, but he also passed on a creative and impulsive personality that had led him to pan for gold in Alaska, seek fame in Hollywood, and come up with about a thousand new business ideas before I was sixteen. He basically turned me into an internally consolidated Cassandra. Able to predict the possible outcomes ahead, but without the necessary attention span or impulse control to see it through.

Some people are born with ADHD, others have ADHD thrust upon them.

Another thing that I got from my father came accidentally, when I was going through a box of his hobby detritus that had been left in the garage. Amongst the discarded lock picks and guitar picks, carving tools and welding gear, were a few bits of his past life in the military. Lock picks were not an unusual item to find in our house, but military memorabilia was. My father had sold any items of value from his previous military service, and those things that could not be turned into dollars to support his family had been burned.

Most of the items I found in the box seemed to have been the type that are misplaced and then forgotten. There were two strips of colored ribbon from Purple Hearts, with the metal missing. A braided blue cord. A bayonet.

There was also an old newspaper article that appeared to be a deliberate keepsake, since it had been laminated, although the paper inside had already begun to yellow. The preserved article described how "Lieutenant Krasnesky" had led his company in a charge up a hill to take an enemy position. After being wounded multiple times, his right arm had been blown up and he had lost his rifle, so he had drawn his pistol with his left hand and continued the charge. He did not stop until his company had seized the hill, and only then had "the Pennsylvanian collapsed due to loss of blood from his injuries."

People often use the phrase, "I'll die on this hill", when they refer to something that they believe strongly in. It is commonly used in a humorous manner to declare a dislike for a particular type of candy, or to support an unpopular story line in a television series. It is less frequently used to express an actual willingness to die in defense of a belief or a cause, and it is almost never spoken of in reference to dying on an actual geological feature, outside of a cinematic presentation.

At eleven years old, I met a man in a newspaper clipping that was literally willing to die on a hill. I was fortunate enough that that man was my father, and that I was able to ask him, "Why?"

His initial response was that he had been ordered to, and that was enough for me when I was eleven. We would talk about that hill again one other time, when I was much older. During that second conversation he explained that it had nothing to do with orders and that he actually thought the orders had been stupid at the time, but that he had a responsibility to his soldiers. He said that if he had not kept going, his company would not have had a leader on that hill and many more of them would have died, and so it doesn't matter how injured you are, when other people need you, you just keep going.

I did not have the knowledge or experience at the time of either of those conversations with my father to understand what that meant. I was too immature to accurately distinguish one hill from another. My takeaway was just that I needed to find a hill, and as we all know, there is never a shortage of hills in the world to die upon, so I spent much of my youth rushing from one hill to the next. Most of the hills that I thought were important turned out to be nothing more than piles of debris from construction projects that would eventually bulldoze over previously held beliefs.

As I began to choose my own battles and as I saw the hills that I had once believed in continue to erode away time after time, I began to search for hills of convenience. As the years passed, the hill itself became less and less important. What I wanted was a fight. Any hill would do. In time that would morph even further into simply wanting to die and hoping that this next hill might be the one.

When I reached that point in my journey, I would understand that my father had lost more than the use of his hand in that attack.

From my mother, I developed a love of books, a longing for knowledge, and a passion for growing things but without the requisite ability to keep things alive. The books were my salvation as a child. When you are poor, a book creates a window that allows you to at least see those things that might otherwise be denied to those without the requisite financial ability. A really good book might even become a doorway and allow you to step into another life, even if it is only in your mind. And when you are alone, a book can become your best friend.

My mother encouraged me to quickly move past Seuss and Scarry and on to Vonnegut and Malory and Orwell as quickly as possible. In that regard, my childhood was curtailed in a manner that was not too dissimilar from No Tail. We both were introduced to worlds that were not designed to shelter the young or the innocent. My mother gave me my first pre-existentialist novel,

Dostoyevsky's "The Idiot" when I was seven. It is still one of my favorite novels, but at seven I did not have enough life experience to fully understand what my mind was trying to process.

When allowed free reign among the library stacks, I would usually gravitate more towards those novels that had strong elements of escapism and fantasy. Anything with a flavor of Arthurian romance and wonder. The pre-doomed hero quickly became my favorite character.

These early influences coalesced into a child that believed that the greatest achievement that could be accomplished in life was to be an ill-fated paladin for good. Reenforced by the Puritanical version of religion that I was exposed to, I was also convinced that goodness required suffering, and that the only way to determine whether or not you were on the right path was to measure the degree of suffering that the path presented to you. The more suffering, the more good.

That misguided desire to be good would eventually turn me into something that good would not have recognized.

III

The box in the garage would come later though. The year after we moved from Chicago to a field in Arkansas, I began school and was introduced to the world of "in" groups, and "out" groups. Although larval in form compared to the adult cliques that would develop later in life when the fully formed asshats emerge from their educational pupation, first grade social structure is not as inclusive as we might want to believe it is, particularly when isolation is encouraged by the adults in the classroom.

You might assume that the isolation had to do with poverty, based on my earlier statement about living in a tent and eating beans, but that would only be partially correct. I was not identifiable as "the poor kid" in school. We were certainly poor. When I showed up to first grade, I brought my new pencil box that I had made myself out of papier mâché. Not because I was into arts and crafts, but because we couldn't afford "store bought" school supplies. The entire school though was in a depressed, rural area that had very little in the way of wealth, so there were a lot of poor kids. I might have been in the bottom ten percent, but poverty alone would not have been the thing that placed a target on my back.

The unforgivable sin that I was guilty of was that I was a smart kid that liked reading. I don't know when I started reading, although if you ask my mother, she will tell you that I started reading en utero. I think at times I was as much a curiosity for my parents as I was a child. Like poking a strange insect with a leaf and seeing what it does, they would hand me books and see what I would do with them.

I loved classic Dr. Seuss. Still do. But circumstances required that I seek more complex literature. My parents constantly encouraged me to push further. Receiving books from them was a little like watching people stretching out their arms in front of them in a dark room, trying to determine how big the room really was.

This approach had its positives and its negatives. The positive was that books gave me access to information that I would not have received otherwise. The negative was that I lacked a frame of reference for much of what I read.

There is a reason that kids read "One Fish, Two Fish" before reading Dostoyevsky's "The Idiot." A child can comprehend what a fish is or how many fish there are or whether it is red or blue, but moral ambiguity and the inherent imbalance in social systems based on monetary accumulation are a little more vague for a five year old to grasp.

So, I showed up for my first day of school with my new box of crayons (the eight pack, not the sixty four pack) in my home-made supply box, and when the other kids wanted to talk about what the very hungry caterpillar was going to eat, I wanted to talk about why hunger existed. I was the only kid in first grade suffering from weltschmerz.

I don't like talking about being that kid for several reasons. The first is obvious. It's kind of cringy. It's a metric that feels like a brag. Telling someone that you are seventy-five inches tall is a metric that just sounds like a statement but telling someone what your IQ is always feels like a boast. And when you never really did anything with it, then it's worse than a brag. It's an admission of failure.

It's also not something that a person earns. Intelligence is not a thing that you do. It's just something that you are born with. It isn't an accomplishment any more than being born tall or being born with blue eyes is an accomplishment. It's just a flip of the genetic coin.

The second main reason that I don't like talking about it is because it is the origin of my separation from people. It was what would lead to my first-grade teacher sticking me in a corner to read by myself so that she didn't have to deal with me. It was what would lead to me spending every morning of my second-grade year picking myself out of the sticker bushes that grew along the side of the cafeteria where bus drop off and pick up was.

And since this is the beginning of the book, I don't want to start out by telling you something about myself that will make you dislike me before we make it through the first chapter. Stick around. There will be plenty of things that I will tell you about myself later that will be more than enough to make you dislike me, but don't let this be the thing that you fixate on.

And if you think that someone being afraid of being disliked for being smart is in itself a humble brag, I would invite you to peruse popular culture for a moment. There are movies out there where the smart person winds up being the hero, but it is almost always framed as a thing that must be overcome.

"...and so in the end, we realized that they were people too, IN SPITE of the fact that they were a nerd."

"...and so in the end, they turned out to be physically capable anyway, IN SPITE of the fact that they were a bookworm."

"...and so in the end, people liked them, IN SPITE of the fact that they were smart."

One of my all-time favorite movie characters is Tyrion Lannister in "Game of Thrones", as portrayed by Peter Dinklage. I am aware from the book that his physical appearance was presented as a thing that must be overcome, but his intelligence was as soundly mocked as was his size. I wouldn't give up that part of myself, but it did not make childhood easy.

I liked regular kid stuff, by the way. I don't want you to think that I didn't. I didn't only like reading. I liked playing kickball and playing on the monkey bars and most of the other stuff that everyone grows up doing. But when you're the odd kid that the teacher puts in the corner all day, it's less likely that someone is going to pick you for their Red Rover team. It's less likely that someone is going to pick you to be their friend.

And I really, intensely want to make a joke about it all right now because this just makes me cringe to write about it this way. It's awkward. Like walking in on someone sitting on the toilet. Or in this case, I guess it's more like you all walking in on me while I am on the toilet. Which is another one of my phobias. Because elementary school bathrooms are as good a place to get beat up as the bushes by the bus stop, in case you didn't know.

But, hey, don't leave just yet. We're not going to spend much more of your time talking about my period of victimhood. We'll get to the part of the book where people stop beating me up and I start killing people soon enough. You'll be able to like me then. Because killing is a lot more acceptable than the shameful sin of being smart.

IV

My second year of school was even less auspicious than the first. It was the year I took up residence in the thorn bushes. The year that adults began to take on a sinister pallor. It was the year that my teacher decided that it was not enough to just ignore me, but that it was necessary to seek out opportunities to publicly embarrass me for the way I thought or the way I dressed, and the year that an elder from our church decided to show me something special in the bathroom. The year that the father of the only kid who would sit next to me on the bus took out his shotgun one day and then suddenly I was sitting by myself again.

It was the year that I began to understand Dostoyevsky.

Eventually, I wound up skipping a grade in school, because it was easier for most teachers to send me to someone else than to figure out how to teach me. Then pretty soon I skipped another grade. We had no gifted and talented program at our school. Just a corner of the room where they could stick me while I read.

Ultimately they skipped me right on out of school altogether and into college.

I was about as ready for college at sixteen as I was ready for Dostoyevsky at six. I had no social skills. No academic skills. No discipline. No goals.

Which is how I wound up losing all of my scholarships in my first year and working in a chicken processing plant. For three years I wandered from job to job, and from major to major, paying for a semester at a time, as my savings account allowed, and at the end of those three years, I joined the Army. People have often asked me why I joined, and I routinely tell them, glibly, by the way, "It was because it was a Tuesday."

It's as good a reason as any. It was a Tuesday. I was skipping class, again, and went into the mall that morning, and wandered into a recruiting office.

With as much thought as I gave most major decisions in my life at that time, I signed up for the Army and was on a bus to the Military Entrance Processing Station that evening.

My parents were not thrilled about my new career path. Their bragging rights had already begun to fade after that first questionable year of college attendance.

"Did I tell you about my genius son?"

"You have another son? The only one that I know about is the one that works in the slaughterhouse? Or is it Walmart now? And what major is he on now? Theater? English? Pre-law? I can never remember."

Fortunately for my parents though, a war broke out, and they were able to recast their college dropout son as a newly minted soldier coin. I spent a few years as an Arabic speaking low-level intercept team leader, before learning that I definitely did not want to spend the next twenty years of my life doing it. I came home, determined to suck it up and finish my degree and go to med school. Or possibly become a priest. Probably one of those two, unless some other new whim came along, but I was definitely NOT going back to the Army. That one thing was certain.

Then I met this girl.

V

She was gorgeous. I mean, like absolutely knock out gorgeous. Like movie star or model or marry a prince of a small European country gorgeous. And smart too. There are plenty of pretty girls in college, and plenty of smart girls in college, but to find one that is a cross between Audrey Hepburn and Claudette Colbert stunning, that is also smart is rare.

But do you wanna know the best part?

She was broken too.

She was so broken that she didn't realize how beautiful she was. I once watched a guy walk straight into a metal light pole because he was staring at her as she walked by. Then, even after he had practically knocked himself out, he was still so enthralled by her that as he picked himself up off the ground, he was turning around to see her go. I pointed it out to her as an example of the impact she had on people, but she dismissed it as "just one of those things that happen." And of course, as the rest of us are aware, if people walking into poles is "just one of those things that happen" when you are around, you are not an average coed.

After meeting her, priesthood was immediately off my list of career choices. Robin frequently tells people that the Catholic church owes her a debt of gratitude for helping to steer me clear of that vocation. She's probably right. I would have made a horrible priest.

I was far too judgmental at that point in my life. Some of you might be thinking, no, that sounds about right for a priest but trust us. It would not have been a good fit.

I had settled too comfortably into the belief that I was usually right, and mostly good. I would not have been an understanding cleric and would have had no tolerance for sin. I would not have been able to separate the sin from the sinner. There was very little about me that was compassionate.

When I met Robin, I finally felt like there was something human about me. I felt like there was a chance that I might not spend my entire life feeling alone.

The psychologist in me feels the need to step in right now and offer a disclaimer. Do not do what we did. Two broken people meeting might sound like the romantic beginning to a John Hughes film, or more likely a Wes Anderson movie, since neither of us were in high school at that point, but this is a bad idea. If you are broken, do not find another broken person. Go get some glue and fix yourself first, and then find someone else that has fixed themselves too.

The idea that broken people can fix broken people was something that some broken person came up with. If we were good at fixing things, we would have fixed ourselves. That is not the way relationships are supposed to work. Relationships are supposed to be like plates. Not necessarily identical but roughly the same size and shape so that when you put them in the cabinet, they stack together neatly. That is how people are supposed to fit together in a relationship. Not like two plates that were dropped on the floor.

Have you ever dropped a plate? I know there's supposed to be this neat romantic notion that "your broken pieces fit my broken pieces, and now together we are whole" but if that is what you believe then please, for the love of Pete, before you try dating, go home and take two plates and drop them on the floor and then see if you can easily fit two halves of different plates together. You can't do it. The edges are sharp and uneven, and you will bloody your fingers trying to make them fit.

But, as Puck observes in "A Midsummer's Night Dream", "What fools these mortals be." So, Robin and I pressed our broken pieces together. And miraculously, we eventually would figure out how to make a complete plate out of our pieces, but we would cut each other on our jagged edges many times before getting there.

The first time that I suggested to Robin that we should go out on a date, she gave me a copy of the Myers-Briggs Type Indicator and asked me to fill it out. And when I say she gave me a copy, I don't mean she said, "You should go online and fill out the MBTI and then tell me what you scored." I mean she reached into her bag and pulled out a paper copy of it and gave it to me, complete with a manila envelope to turn it back in to her for grading. I dislike being labeled and have told her many times that I considered not filling it out, but the truth is that I did not hesitate. I would have filled out the MMPI extended version if it meant I could take her to dinner.

Two weeks after our first date, I bought a ring. Two weeks after that, I proposed.

She never actually said yes. Her response was, "Okay." She might have referenced my Psycho-deviate score on the MMPI as well, but she didn't say no, and so we got married. As part of the natural progression of being non-priested, we had two children. I completed my degree and eventually found myself as a teacher in a rural school in Arkansas. Then came 9/11. And I wound up doing that thing that I said I would never do again.

VI

In 2003, I went into the looking glass.

That is how I occasionally refer to my second deployment to Iraq. As Yeats might say, it was where the center lost its hold, and things started to fall apart. It was where life grinned at you and then winked out, disappearing like an amused Cheshire cat, and heads rolled, but it wasn't the red queen that was doing the executions.

On the morning of September 11th, 2001, my principal came down the hall and said, "I think you need to come to the library and see this. Now."

Thirty-three days later, on October 14th, 2001, I was back in uniform as part of a voluntary recall to active duty. Two years later, in 2003, I was the battalion intelligence officer for the main effort of the ground forces in the province of Diyala.

For the next year, I would average less than four hours of sleep a night and would participate in almost three hundred raids and combat operations. Sometimes my team and I would come back in from one operation only to turn around at the gate and roll right back out with another unit that was already staged and ready to go. It was during this time that Captain Nabil was born.

I told you initially that I was born in Chicago, but perhaps it would be more accurate to call Baqubah my place of birth. Not quite Afghanistan, but I was drawing closer to that cat that I had not yet met. Captain Nabil was a necessary tool that developed organically when a situation arose where it was more convenient to use an Arabic name than an English one. Nabil was the name that I had gone by during my earlier language training, and I was a captain at that point in my career, so Captain Nabil was an easy mantle to assume.

What had started out as a necessity became something of a game. I started to leave Kilroy style messages after raids that said, "Captain Nabil was here." I would tell sources to spread the word that Captain Nabil was looking for someone, and then when that someone disappeared…poof, it was Captain Nabil. It was an absolute gas to me the first time I heard about Captain Nabil getting credit for something that I hadn't even been involved in. The ultimate, of course, was the first time that I found out that there was a bounty out for "Captain Nabil."

That was a hoot. What a knee-slapper.

Robin, however, did not find this development amusing.

VII

The life of a military spouse is often glorified, and even revered at times, but the reality of it is far from what can be contained in an emotional four-minute song, or a photo montage at a retirement ceremony, which is usually the version that most people not in the military are exposed to. When they want to try to be real, they might call it "gritty", but they'll say it in a way that clearly implies it's supposed to be kind of cool, but it isn't.

It isn't gritty in the way that we think of something that is tough, but enduring. It is gritty in the way that sand is when it gets into your bathing suit and you have a four hour car ride ahead of you to get home from the beach but the air conditioning has gone out in the car and so you buy an ice cream to cool you off but it melts and drips into your lap and now you have sand and sticky dairy product in uncomfortable places that you do not want sand and sticky dairy product in. That is the kind of gritty that being a military spouse is.

I had the luxury of access to communication equipment that not everyone had at that time, and I would call home frequently to talk to Robin and the girls. The first time one of our conversations was interrupted by gunfire and I had to duck below the edge of a building because someone was shooting at me, the military spouse experience quickly lost its glamor and romance. I learned that the things that I thought were funny, like an IED attack that didn't go off, or a mortar that sent shrapnel through the chair you had been sitting in seconds before, were somehow not that funny to the people that you had left behind.

Honestly, I think it was often more real for her than it was for me. I was the one in it, but "it" was "through the looking glass." "It" wasn't real. It was this twisted dimension where people wanted to kill some guy named Captain Nabil, and that definitely wasn't me, was it? Why would people want to kill ME? That couldn't be real. And by the way, did you hear the one about the guy who was decapitated? It's hilarious. It'll make you piss your pants. But it's definitely not real.

Do you want to know what is real?

Two nights before we deployed, while a lot of people were getting drunk, Robin and I took the kids to Barnes and Noble, and we ran into a friend who had also brought his family there to attempt to create some sense of normalcy before the chaos ahead of us. Six months later, that friend was on a patrol when they were attacked. He did everything right. Had all of his gear on and did what he was supposed to do, and he was one of the good guys, but it didn't matter. A piece of shrapnel caught him in the neck, above his protective collar. A thousand to one possibility. And then he was gone.

Robin took our two daughters to the memorial service that was held for him in Texas. I attended the memorial service that was held in country. After the service, I spoke with Robin and my girls on the phone. My youngest was worried because her friend's father wasn't coming home, and so from my land of make-believe, I told her that I promised her that I would come home. Her response to me was, "I bet Ria's dad promised her that too."

And that is real.

Because I got to hang up the phone and return to Wonderland and the make-believe world of the Mad Hatter and Captain Nabil, who, rumor has it, found the person responsible for the attack that killed my friend, but Robin had to ride home from that memorial service, with two scared children, and she was the one that had to hold them when they cried because they weren't afraid of a monster in the closet like kids at that age should be. They were afraid of a monster that had eaten one of their friends dads, and that monster was still hungry.

That's not gritty. That is real and that is terrifying.

And there were so many memorials.

VIII

I came home from that deployment. I was damaged, but I was home, which was more than could be said for a lot of my friends. Then, in 2007, a presidential election campaign was beginning to swing into action, and my righteous outrage was about to land me in a world of trouble.

Three things converged one evening in July, which would put me on a path that would eventually intersect with a cat that was less than a year away from being born. Those three things were my choice to watch the news, a position paper about Iraq that I had written a few months earlier, and a set of old dishes.

Three years into our war in Iraq, I had become frustrated with the lack of progress that was being made. I wrote a five-page paper, outlining five key points that I felt would put things on a path that was both equitable and positive. The points that I made in the paper were almost embarrassingly simple, and I was certain that there had to be someone at higher echelons of government that had thought of these things, but since things were where they were, perhaps the obvious was being missed. I had sent the paper out to several key individuals that I thought might benefit from an outside set of eyes, but I had received no response.

I had also recently started to declutter some of the items that had accumulated in our storage unit, and had created an Ebay account to list them, and hopefully sell them. Such an inconsequential thing would have a disproportionately huge consequence.

The third thing was, I made the mistake of watching the news. I highly recommend against watching news unless you have been advised by your doctor to find sedentary ways to increase your blood pressure and add ungodly levels of stress and frustration to your life. There was a debate going on and everyone had points to make, and they were all passionately talking about the numbers of deaths so far, some of them inflating them, some of them deflating them, some of them dismissing them, but with everyone it was just numbers, numbers, numbers. These people that these numbers represented had been reduced to nothing more than a tool to manipulate people to think one way or another. There was no humanity there. Only statistics.

For someone that had attended the memorial services for these numbers-that-were-no-longer-people, it was obscene.

So, there I was, morally outraged, with an Ebay account, and a five-page solution to the war in Iraq.

Why not? This seemed like as good a hill as any.

Now you might think that listing the solution to the war in Iraq on Ebay would elicit a humorous chuckle from an organization like the military that is known for its sense of jocularity, and is never heavy-handed or authoritarian in its reaction to a mentally unstable but in a childish way, captain, who would have been better served developing a drinking problem than opening up his Ebay account that night. You might even think that politicians who are always clearly open-minded and interested in hearing points of view that might differ from their own, as long as it brings a problem closer to resolution would have been intrigued by the offer. The response, however, was less amused and open-minded than one might hope.

At the time that what has become known in our family as "The Ebay incident" occurred, I had already been selected for a competitive program that allowed a dozen officers every year to complete a master's degree at Columbia University. After the incident, however, my orders for Columbia were revoked, and I was given new orders to deploy to Iraq for the third time instead. I was assured that it was not punitive. The old turnip "needs of the Army" was trotted out. They needed me. They weren't punishing me.

Unfortunately, my "non-punishment" didn't just impact me. It impacted my family. And yeah, initially it might elicit a chuckle to think of someone impulsively acting out in an incongruously ridiculous manner like that. The solution to a war being listed on Ebay is comical in its absurdity. But when you think of a family being left once again. And you think of the phone calls. And the memorials. So many memorials. All of those numbers with names that caused the initial outrage.

Suddenly it's not so funny anymore.

So, in 2008, at the same time that a certain black kitten was being born in Afghanistan, instead of packing my notebooks for Columbia, I was packing my duffle bags for Iraq. Rumor has it, Captain Nabil would be joining me on this trip too.

IX

There are many important aspects of team building and for $24.95 you can probably find a thousand books about it online. Most of them get parts of it right and parts of it wrong. The reason that there isn't a single solution for how to build a team is that there is more than one team. If the world only had one team, then one book would suffice, but every team is different.

An important part of the team building process in the military is coming up with a name for the team. We're big on names in the military. The more threatening and scarier they are, the better. Back in my enlisted days, when I was a low-level team leader, the Army officially called our team "Black Death." I suppose that was supposed to be motivational, but intel people are built differently. We thought it was stupid, and chose our own name, so although the official plaques and papers all referred to us as "Black Death," the name that we used in our own paperwork and in our briefings, and the name that we stenciled onto our gear with the regulation army stencils and paint was, "The Chocolate Milkmen."

In 2008, the year that I was definitely NOT being punished, the team that I trained with and deployed with went through the usual cycle of recommendations for names like, Team Overkill, and Team Kickass, and basically a lot of variants on the general theme of naming something to indicate that our penises were magically larger than the penises of our enemies.

Damn. Team Magic Penis. How did we miss that one?

Anyway, after lengthy discussions, the name that we chose was Team Shepherd. We decided that it was more important that we focus on finding ways to help people than in flexing our reproductive might. From 2008 to 2009, during the first year of No Tail's life, while he was being hunted by the misguided animal extermination squads in Afghanistan, I was back in Iraq with

Team Shepherd, working with Iraqi intelligence units, and meeting Dogulus, a young female mutt that lived on an Iraqi compound we visited, and Leighton and Lenore, two young spotted cats that lived underneath my hut along the Diyala River.

Upon my return from that deployment, I received the positive news that Columbia had deferred my acceptance into their master's program. I spent the next year studying psychology and leadership, and although I seemed capable of making friendships in combat situations, I once again found myself struggling to develop relationships when bullets weren't involved.

Social situations often make me uncomfortable. Not in the PTSD kind of "I-can't-relax" way, but in the "I feel like an alien and I'm not sure how to react" way. I can dissect it rationally when I separate the situation from the self. When you are separated from your classmates at six, you do not organically develop the social muscles necessary to fit in. Being a fifteen-year-old senior in high school does not lend itself to casual integration. Being poor multiplies the effect exponentially.

With that background, every subsequent gathering or social interaction begins to feel the way you felt when you were a kid and you were tucked into the same set of "nice clothes" for three seasons, regardless of how much you had grown or how the black, plastic shoes pinched and crushed your toes, or how the grey, JC Penney's suit chafed parts of you that were gradually becoming aware that they did not like to be chafed.

The majority of my social understanding was garnered academically, like any other course of study. It made me successful in those situations that favor artificiality. Say for instance, when you need to unobtrusively fit in in a coffee shop in Buhriz. Authenticity though makes me uncomfortable.

The time I spent at Columbia was an amazing academic experience, but away from the battlefield, I became socially more isolated. There were a couple of students that I bonded with and felt close to, but whenever there were group activities, I felt my toes getting pinched. The too-small suit of building relationships chafed.

The thing that saved me during that period at Columbia, and what would continue to save me for years to come was one of my professors. All of the professors I encountered there were outstanding, but there was one in particular. Pretty sure she was on loan from one of the magical schools, like that place in Britain with the dragons. She was the perfect blend of wisdom and humor, with just enough of mean in her to let you know she meant business. After an episode of social dysfunction that was more obvious than most, she followed me outside after class and confronted me with a very blunt and unambiguous declaration.

"You have PTSD. You need to go to therapy."

It wasn't delivered with a soft voice and a caring touch. It wasn't polite, but her intent was not to be polite. Her intent was to help, and although her observation was harsh, it was also full of love.

She could have just let it go and said nothing. I would have deserved it.

The statement itself did not come as a surprise. The program I was in was a psychology program after all. I knew I had PTSD. It was not an eye-opening revelation for me. And I was even an advocate for people seeking therapy. I just didn't see it as the best fit for me, for several reasons.

I explained to the professor that I could not go to therapy, because it would impact my clearance. Although, technically, the Army could not pull someone's clearance at that time and list "PTSD" as the reason, it was not uncommon for auxiliary issues to be cited as the cause a clearance was downgraded. She then told me that in that case I should seek counseling outside of the military system. I informed her that without the military insurance, I could not afford a therapist. She responded by giving me her office contact number and telling me to schedule an appointment, free of charge.

2009 was a year of reprieve for No Tail and me. For No Tail, it was the year that they rescinded the animal termination policy on the base where he lived. For me, it was the year that a psychology professor reached out to me after class. The result of these actions was that both of us would continue to live.

Over the next year, the professor and I began to catalog my numerous injuries, just like the veterinary care team were cataloging No Tail's injuries, eight thousand miles away. The list grew for both of us every time we were treated. His folder was in a moving container turned into an office in Kabul. My folder was in a wooden file drawer in a small office just west of Central Park. I pulled up my metaphorical sleeves and showed the professor my scars. The friends that had been lost. The children I had held. The injustices I had witnessed. The rage that had grown.

And the shadows. We would spend a lot of time talking about the shadows.

X

Neither of these reprieves though, were long lived. No Tail and I both had a tendency to engage in activities that were self-destructive. I don't know that the worst of either of our injuries were fully our own faults, but I am certain that we did not help the matter.

For my part, the professional chastisements and counselings would begin to pile up. It was not long after leaving Columbia that I would get reprimanded for not "making" Robin attend a tea that was being thrown by the general's wife.

Okay.

Technically, I was reprimanded for my response to a senior officer when he implied that Robin had a responsibility to support the Army mission. I probably could have chosen better words when I told him that I was the one that had signed up for the military and that my wife hadn't signed up for anything, so if he had anything constructive to say about my own performance I would be happy to listen but that Robin would attend or not attend teas as she saw fit, and I would not be hearing my wife's name come up in another of my performance reviews again. Ever.

Another senior officer also made the mistake of making an improper comment about Robin, and I made him come to my house to discuss the matter. I told him that he had two choices. He could apologize to Robin personally and immediately, or he could step into the backyard to have a discrete and personal discussion with me. If he chose not to apologize, or if he chose to run away, I informed him that I would call JAG and file charges against him before he had time to make it back to his office and complain to the general about me.

It was not long after that that I was transferred.

Was I standing up for my wife? Sure. But let's not make it more noble than it really was. I was still leaping from hill to hill, looking for the one that I could die on. I was right, but I wasn't noble.

In my new roll, after the transfer, I was once again in a position where I was the subject matter expert for intelligence issues, part of which encompassed interrogation and detention procedures. But there was another hill, and another professional conflict, and the long arms of the old boy's network reached out once again to tap me on the shoulder for my fourth deployment. This time it was Afghanistan.

I pointed out that I was an Arabic linguist and Middle Eastern specialist. I did not speak any Afghan dialects of Urdu, or Pashto, or Farsi. The response I got was the equivalent of a shoulder shrug and the attitude that one Muslim country was the same as the next.

As deployments go, the fourth one barely counted. It was less than three months long and consisted primarily of working in a detention facility in Bagram. Most of my time there was nothing more than in-country research. The final product that I had compiled was a report that covered ten years of operations in theater. Things we had done right, things we had done wrong, and places where we could improve.

I was still assigned to a stateside unit, and my commander was stateside as well. My place of duty just happened to be in Afghanistan. As I was preparing to leave theater, an in-theater senior officer informed me that I could not leave until he had "approved" my final report.

I told him that I didn't work for him and that I was going to release my report with or without his approval. After holding me there for a couple of days, my stateside commander capitulated and told me to let him review the report. Upon reviewing it, he ordered me to delete those things that made our operations look less than flattering, but that I could keep the things in that made us look good.

I told him that the point of the report was not to make us look good or to look bad. Optics was irrelevant. It was an internal document that was ultimately there for the purpose of saving lives. I was once again told that I would be held there in Afghanistan until the necessary changes had been made.

Now technically, the report was already done and could be published on high-side, classified networks. I had not done so yet because I was waiting to return home to do it, but there was no reason that I could not use in-theater systems to publish it. So, I did.

The senior official was not particularly pleased about my choice, but it did at least remove his objection to my going home.

The next assignment would be even worse.

I worked for a commander that made several improper comments about women and minorities. For some reason, I still thought that doing the right thing would result in the right results, so I reported him. To be clear, he did this multiple times. I had counseled him privately and had warned him that what he was saying was inappropriate, just in case he had slept through the hundreds of briefings about this exact thing.

He did not curb his behavior, so in keeping with the stated values of the military, I reported him. The investigation quickly revealed that, even with the fear of reprisal hanging over the unit, there were others that were willing to come forward and confirm the allegations I had made. Still, it dragged on, which made for an incredibly charged work environment. The end result was that the offending officer was reassigned but not punished. And I was given the option to go on my fifth deployment.

This was not as punitive as it might sound, but it wasn't NOT punitive either. It was a compromise. My younger daughter was a junior in high school. She had at this point in her life lived in five different states and attended multiple schools. Robin and I wanted to do whatever we could to give her the option of stabilizing for her last two years of high school and graduating with her friends.

The compromise was that I agreed to go away so that everyone did not have to stand around and stare at me awkwardly, and in return for agreeing to the deployment, the military would guarantee that I could remain in place for the two years Isabelle would need to finish school.

The military agreed. Robin accepted. The kids cried. And I packed my bags.

No Tail and I Meet

One more goodbye, one more farewell,

One more soul in heaven, one more empty place in hell.

One more letter home, one more folded flag,

One more remnant of a life packed in one more duffle bag.

I don't know what my life has in store,

But I'm too tired to handle one more.

From the musical **"Babylon"**, by Thad Krasnesky

BERT

I

The deployment started out on a less than auspicious note. I was originally slated to be the intel advisor for a Special Operations group. It was at least going to be an interesting assignment I thought, with a lot of opportunities for dynamic engagements. When I arrived in country, however, there was no one to greet me at the airfield in Bagram. I had to wrangle all five duffle bags full of gear while somchow trying to find out where the Special Operations office on the base was.

It would have made a great Monty Python skit. Wandering from office to office, asking if anyone knew where the secret office was. Adding to this sweaty comedy routine would have been my response when people would ask me who I was.

"I'm the new special ops intelligence officer."

"And you're going to be in charge of finding the bad guys?"

"Yeah, that's me."

"But you don't know where your own office is?"

I did eventually find the Special Ops group, but they were as surprised to see me as I was to have not been picked up at the airfield. They had been waiting on a new intel officer for a while but when a replacement had not been forthcoming, they had decided to attach an officer from another unit that was already in theater. When you're Special Ops, you can do stuff like that. So, the assignment that I was there to fill had already been filled.

It took several hours for me to finally get in contact back in the states with my assignment branch, at which point they explained the error by saying, "Whoopsie."

They said that they would get things sorted out soon, but for now I was to "sit tight" which meant that me and my five bags of gear had to shuffle along to temporary housing, and then show back up at the office the following day at nine.

At nine, there was still no assignment. I contemplated simply getting back on a plane and flying home. I had not yet been attached to a unit so the question of needing a release from theater was ambiguous at best. Technically, I wouldn't be violating any rules by doing so, and if they didn't need me there, I had no desire to be there.

It was the absolute worst wallflower situation I had ever been in. It's one thing to stand on the side at a school dance, but when there's a war on and the music's playing and you still haven't been asked out on the floor, it makes you feel like maybe it was a waste of your time polishing your shoes for this in the first place.

At five o'clock that evening though, an assignment finally came through. I was going to Kabul to be the Director of the Combined Joint Intelligence Operations Center – NATO, or CJIOC-N, for short. I was not thrilled about this. Anything that has "director" in the title implied that I was going to be spending more time behind a desk than I would like. Also, as a rule of thumb, the more initials an organization has, the less it actually does. And putting me in Kabul, next to the embassy, meant that I was going to have to do a lot of coordinating and saluting. Not the best gig for someone that occasionally does not play well with others.

Still, without other options available to me, I showed up at the flight line and boarded the plane.

11

It was getting dark when the chopper landed on the rugby field that evening. It was April in Kabul, which meant that it was still chilly out, and to top off the evening, it had just begun to rain. A couple of soldiers came out to the chopper and grabbed my bags and carried them to the side of the field where a Humvee was waiting, along with my new commander. He introduced himself to me and then told me to take my bags to my room and then come and see him at the SCIF once I had deposited my bags.

Remember those decrepit, moldy trailers that I mentioned earlier?

That was where I would spend the first few weeks of my new life in Kabul. I wrangled my bags through the tight halls and to the room that I had been assigned. Since I was the new guy in the room, my bed was the small, angled bunk that was wedged into the top corner of the room. With that enjoyable task complete, I followed my guide back across the base to the SCIF.

There was a large metal gate that led into the entrance area of the building. It had a very "Mad Max" feel to it. Oversized for its purpose, like it was intended to intimidate instead of secure. As the door swung open, I was greeted not by a person in uniform, but by a sleek, black cat.

I was an intelligence officer, and we are trained to notice things like this, so with fifteen years of experience behind me, I authoritatively stated, "There's a cat."

The escort that had brought me to the building was obviously not impressed with my analytical ability. It seemed he had already come to the same conclusion and was aware there was a cat there.

"That's No Tail," he said.

That was it. That was all the explanation that I was given as to why there was a cat in what was supposed to be a secured facility. The escort continued on to the interior door, and I followed. No Tail turned his head, the only part of him that moved as he watched us pass.

For those that were hoping for a more dramatic first meeting, you are going to be disappointed. There wasn't a moment of instant bonding where a warm-hearted cat recognized a damaged soldier and leapt into my arms to help me learn to feel again. There wasn't even a grudging acknowledgment of two kindred souls, exchanging wounded but knowing glances as we realized that our lives were about to become inseparably intertwined.

I don't think that I even attempted to pet him that first night. I wasn't in the best of moods, after having played musical assignments over the last two days. As far as No Tail was concerned, I didn't have any food with me, so I was of no interest or use to him. We passed like two angry ships in the night.

I was taken through the facility and introduced to the staff. Part of my job would require that I come to this facility twice a day to exchange information and brief the different commanders that were involved in operations, and occasionally even brief the ambassador or visiting politicians or dignitaries.

Politicians and dignitaries?

Oh, yes. What you think is about to happen, happened. But you'll have to wait for that.

After the orientation to the main facility, I was taken across the compound to my office. My office was also a SCIF, but it was not quite as well maintained. We were on the low-rent side of the intel world apparently.

In that office complex, I was introduced to the team that I would work with for the next seven months, and it was where I almost immediately discovered how good and how bad things were about to get. The good part was the people. They were some absolutely incredible intelligence officers and even better people. We had officers from twelve different countries on our team, and we were responsible for coordinating with twenty more. In rank, they ranged from junior lieutenants to mid-level majors. The bad part was that, as the senior major and the representative of the US contingent, I was their commander.

III

The best news I received my first week in country was when they informed me that my title was technically "Chief" of CJIOC-NATO, and not "Director". That didn't change the job of course, but the title at least didn't make me feel like I needed to wear polyester and call people "Sport," and say things like, "The monthly reflexive calcitrations are less optimified per our quota for unresponsive process funging."

The rest of the week went downhill from there. It was full of unresponsive funging.

I had an unrealistic and unfounded hope that my job would be a beautiful carousel of interwoven and seamless intelligence operations, with possibly some singing along the way, and hopefully even a cameo appearance from Julie Andrews. A coordinated effort among allies. What I found out was that my job was not only bureaucratic. It was meta-bureaucratic. Not only did I have to deal with the unwieldiness of American decomparmentalization, but I had to multiply that times twenty. It seems that governments everywhere may not be united in their desire to share intelligence and work together, but they are absolutely united in their belief that the more ineffective layers you can create between the decision makers and the people doing the work, the better.

It was a nightmare. Every report had to be screened for clearance from the incoming country, and then distribution could only occur after information had been scrubbed based on the clearance of the receiving country. Briefings had to be rewritten based on whether this ambassador or that general was going to be in attendance. It was like being in a room with fifty people, where every person in the room was given three or four pieces of a puzzle, and they could only share those pieces with certain other people in the room, and even the rules that governed what could be shared were secret.

German commander: "We are going to maneuver through this village on our way up the valley, and...."

Me: "I wouldn't go through that village if I were you."

German commander: "Why?"

Me: "I can't tell you. It's a secret."

Australian commander: "Why is it a secret?"

Me: "Listen, Australia. As far as you're concerned, I can't even tell you that this village exists."

Lithuanian commander: *Still standing out in the hall, staring at his watch and wondering when we are going to let him in.*

You would think that post-9-1-1, we would have gotten better about sharing information. We have, to a degree, but mostly what we've gotten better at is hosting interdepartmental mixers, while still hoarding the nuggets of information in our caverns of proprietary knowledge. For someone that has a history of not always keeping their opinions to themselves, this was not an ideal assignment, and would lead to an almost catastrophic conclusion seven months later.

IV

I did not see No Tail on my next trip to the main SCIF, but I did see the feeding station that had been set up for him under the bench in the entrance. I asked about the cat that I had seen the night before and was told that most of the cats on the base stayed in their own territories but that, "No Tail goes wherever No Tail wants to go." The intelligence center wasn't really a home base for him, but he did spend more time there than he did at most other locations. I learned that he had been there for seven years and had become something of a mascot for the facility. Civilians who cycled through the base on six-month rotations every two years said that seeing No Tail again was one of the biggest positives about the assignment.

It was a few more days before I saw him again. I have always been involved in animal work of one form or another throughout my life, and so when I did see him, I adopted the standard "new cat approach" technique and attempted to make his acquaintance. My slow movements and sweet talking did nothing to win him over though, and he quickly departed the area. Everyone assured me that I shouldn't expect anything from him, but that if I was willing to be patient, I might eventually get him to let me give him a treat or even touch him.

I was not willing to be patient, and I had no desire to develop yet another relationship with an animal that I would have to leave behind. Besides, there were plenty of other cats on the base, and if I felt the need for the peace that physical contact with another creature offered, I would find one that was less finicky. Peace was not my goal. Patience was not my goal. I was in pure survival mode at that point. I was on a deployment that was the lowest physical risk that I had ever experienced, but I was at my most vulnerable.

I was as fragile as I had ever been. Fragile may seem like an odd term to describe a soldier, particularly someone who runs ultra-marathons, plays rugby, and engages in hand-to-hand combat, but my physical ability was not what was at risk of breaking. Mentally I was struggling. Depression coated everything that I experienced. It was like someone had handed me one of those puzzles with the little metal coils that are twisted together, and you have to figure out how to separate them but had made me put on large rubber gloves and thick, distorted goggles first. Everything that I saw or felt was muffled by that layer of depression.

Some people say that they don't like using condoms during sex because it dulls their experience. Well depression makes living your life kind of like having sex with a hundred layers of condoms on. You have the impression that you might be there, but you can't really feel much. Life has no climax.

Anxiety and paranoia also took their toll. There is a saying, "It's not paranoia if they're really out to get you." Well, once you've actually had your name on a wanted poster, distrust seems warranted.

And then of course, there were the hallucinations. The shadows.

So that is what I mean when I say "fragile."

The padding that I wrapped around myself to pack my fragile mental state away to keep it safe in its little box, was finding ways to help. Without that padding I just careened off the walls of the box as life delivered me from one unwanted address to the next, getting more and more broken along the way. With that padding, by finding opportunities to help other people, I was at least able to avoid the worst of the damage.

During other deployments I had found opportunities to do toy drives or build schools or rescue kids or something that was more meaningful than the pointless life of spilling khaki colored blood on a beige battlefield. On previous deployments, I was fortunate enough to have commander's that didn't stop to ask "why." They just said, "Sure. Why not?'

This was not the case this time though. I was too close to the flagpole, as the military expression goes. Any suggestion that I came up with was met with "How does that contribute to your mission?"

"Keeping me sane" was not a response that I could offer, and so my suggestions and requests were denied.

Toy drive?

Denied.

Chess club for kids?

Denied.

Over and over again, any attempt to carve out a self that was not wholly defined by the uniform was turned down. Then I happened to notice the live traps around the base. I made a few inquiries and discovered the veterinary support team that had been operating on the base for the last six years. They had two full time staff members, but the rest of the team were all volunteers. The best part of it, for me at least, was that it was an existing, pre-approved organization. I didn't need permission to join. All I had to do was sign up.

The team was not much different from other animal rescue groups I have worked with. Small, understaffed, overworked, but passionate. Contrary to what people who have not worked in animal rescue might believe, the majority of your volunteer time is mundane and administrative. You don't spend your days playing with cats and dogs. The time that you spend with the animals is mostly the routine stuff like cleaning litter boxes and changing out food and water bowls. The few moments that you do get to pet them and play with them is worth it though.

One of the main tasks that volunteers were needed for on the base was setting and checking the live traps around the base. I had worked with live traps extensively before, and with my running schedule this was a task that I could easily fit into my day without interfering with other duties. It was also a volunteer task that allowed me to support the group without requiring much interaction on my part with other volunteers. So, my second week in country, I became a member of the group that called themselves the Feline Conservation Corps.

There were about thirty cats that were being actively monitored on the base at the time I joined the FCC. The officer in charge of the unit would set up a schedule for when each cat needed a checkup, or when a new cat was reported in an area, or when a current track hadn't been seen in a while, and he would then direct us to set up the live traps in a designated grid that would allow them to gather the information that was needed.

It was during my third week in country that I would have my first meaningful interaction with No Tail, and it was not a positive one.

V

My third week in country started out with good news. A space in the newer residential buildings opened up, and I was able to move from the cramped, District 12 quarters in the asbestotic trailers to the chic, two-person rooms where I only had to share a bathroom with a few dozen people, and the floors didn't threaten to collapse underneath you. I also got my first capture in one of the live traps.

I had set the trap the previous evening, shortly before going to bed. The following morning, I got up early to run, as was my usual routine. I chose a route through the base that allowed me to check my trap, as well as the two other traps that had been set by other volunteers.

As I completed the stretch along the northern edge of the compound, I began to hear a sound. I assumed it was a cat because it was the only thing in my sound memory that came close to what I was hearing. What it sounded most like was what I might imagine the unholy offspring of a World War II air raid siren and a blue whale might sound like if they were able to mate, but since Afghanistan is landlocked, the blue whale part was highly unlikely, so my best guess was "cat."

As I got closer, I picked up my pace. I was becoming concerned that the animal I was hearing, whether it was indeed a cat, or the improbably siren-whale hybrid, might be injured. It didn't sound injured though. It didn't sound like it was getting ready to fight, or like it was frightened. I am familiar with many different types of animal speech, and this was something wholly new. I considered that it was simply one of the more common animal emotions but was being communicated in the animal version of Pashto. Maybe I could speak English cat and Arabic cat, but perhaps this was Afghan cat dialect that I had yet to learn.

The closest thing to what I was hearing that I could think of was anger. At volumes that were hard to comprehend certainly, but still it was anger.

The reason that it took me a moment to process it and comprehend what the emotion was that I was hearing, was because it was not the type of anger that I am used to hearing from animals. This was not territorial threatening, or posturing over resources, or even the dangerous sounds that are made when an animal's intent is to kill. This was something harder. Something strange, but with a familiarity to it that made it frustrating to not be able to classify it.

Then I finally placed it, and it struck me why it had been so hard to place the emotion that I was hearing. The anger that I heard had a human note to it. Animal anger can be dangerous but even in its darkest moment there is usually a recognizable degree of purity in it. There is usually purpose behind it. Anger in humans though is often nothing more than anger for its own sake. It is not situational. It is a characteristic. And hearing a degree of sentient, purposeful human anger woven into the instinctual howl of a cat created something unnerving and unnatural.

It was disturbing.

I turned toward the gazebo where I had placed the trap and finally saw the source of the sound. Thankfully, it was just a cat. I had discarded the siren-whale hybrid as an option for the source of the sound, but I had started to consider that perhaps the tuna I had used in the trap had been some sort of holy tuna and that I might have trapped some minor-level demon with a thing for seafood, so I was pleased to see that it was just a cat because I didn't know where to find a priest at this time of the morning.

As soon as No Tail saw me approaching, his shouts changed. They were no longer generalized howls of rage. They were now specific threats against me, my family, and everything that I loved and held dear. If he had to destroy the entire world to do it, he would make me pay for this injustice that I had visited upon him.

I approached the cage like I was approaching an IED made from a dozen howitzer shells, daisy-chained together, that I had to defuse. From the look I was receiving from the cat inside, I think I would have been safer with the IED. I could practically see the little cartoon tendrils of fuming vitriol rising off of him.

I quickly recognized the cat inside as No Tail, for obvious reasons, but whether or not he recognized me in that moment was unclear. His demeanor did not change as I approached the trap, and I was faced with a new dilemma. The trap had a carrying handle on top of it, as most of them do, but to carry it comfortably requires carrying it the way you would a briefcase or gym bag.

With the handle in your hand, a normal posture would place the cage alongside your leg.

This did not seem like a wise thing to do. Even had I been wearing a suit from the bomb disposal squad, I don't know that it could have withstood the claws that lashed out through the bars of the cage. Since I was wearing running shorts, I suspected that if I attempted to carry the trap normally, the skin on my legs would quickly resemble a tattered and shredded picnic bench awning that had been left outside for too many seasons, and I would likely die from blood loss before I ever got back to the FCC office.

To avoid an ignominious death, I was forced to carry the cage with my arm extended away from my body, which is fine for the first few minutes, but a twelve pound cat and a ten pound cage began to feel progressively heavier when carried in this manner, especially when the cat inside is rushing back and forth and leaping from side to side with such force that you expect the wire to give way at any moment. I had to set the cage down to rest more than once on the trip. No Tail used this extended period of time to list all of the generations of my descendants that would suffer for this outrage.

We eventually made it to the FCC facility, and I was able to turn No Tail over to another volunteer. The other volunteer was familiar with No Tail.

"Tuna?" they asked.

It turned out that No Tail was not caught as frequently as other cats on the base because his palate was more discerning than the other cats. There was regular cat food placed around the base at the authorized feeding stations, so he was not about to enter a trap for something that he could just get anywhere. He even disregarded the more enticing cans that were occasionally used to bait a trap to draw in the more reticent felines for check-ups. But put tuna in a trap and he would walk in every time, knowing full well that he was about to be trapped.

I read his file and listened to the other volunteer fill me in on his history. He began to become more than just a name to me. I saw page after page of injuries in his folder. Heard about his two-year disappearance.

Maybe that was where it began. Where I started to see something in this cat that I understood. I have a weakness for broken things. An affinity for what has been discarded. Like calls to like. The broken and discarded know their own. And for a moment there, I was a hungry five-year-old kid again, and what I saw in the cage was an injured kitten. But then the pain and rejection and disappointment had grown over time until it had collapsed down under its own weight to form a gravitational sink of rage.

We might have started bonding then. Perhaps you think that this is where I tell you about how I hung around the facility that morning to speak to No Tail and try to befriend him, or that, after learning about his fondness for tuna, I would sneak some from the mess hall at lunch and come back later in the day to give him a treat.

What happened was the opposite. His story and his anger felt too familiar to me, and I decided that there were plenty of other cats on the base that I could befriend if I felt the need. This one was dangerous in ways that transcended claws and teeth. I sensed that this one had the ability to shred my soul if I let him get too close much more thoroughly than he could have shredded my leg on our trip to the clinic. I resolved to stay away.

No Tail had not let off swearing this entire time, and he informed me that staying away was fine with him. Getting close was not going to be a problem. I left him in the cage there and went back to my room. I showered and went to my office. When I saw No Tail again a few days later in his usual spot under the bench at the intelligence center, we did not speak to each other, and the only eye contact he offered me was a threatening glower.

VI

No Tail was not the only cat on the base, so there were plenty of other options available for me to befriend and pet. Cats that did not take effort. Cats that I could pet and feed and avoid bonding with. Cats that I could treat more like people.

I am generally more successful at building relationships with animals than I am with people. I can become more closely bonded to a stray dog or a wild raccoon or even a traveling crow than I can with people.

Part of it is simply the effort I put in. If I see a wild animal, I will take my time, talk softly to it, move slowly, bring it treats. You can't explain to them what your intent is, so you have to demonstrate it to them.

I tend not to take my time with people. Supposedly, people are sentient creatures so my belief is that I shouldn't have to demonstrate to them my intent. I forget that people are animals too.

In intelligence operations, when a person is a subject, it is easier to treat them like an animal. And I don't mean in the negative, Abu Ghraib kind of way. I don't use the term to indicate poor treatment. I mean that it is easier to treat them as a thing to be understood.

"Othering" is a term that has begun to grow in popular usage over the last several years. Its usage may be new, but it is Hegelian in origin, with the idea being that for us to be aware of ourselves as a distinct individual it is also necessary to identify that there are others who are not ourselves. There is us, and there is "other."

As people, we like to like ourselves, therefore anything that we can more closely identify with ourselves is easier for us to like. Others that are not like us are strange, and therefore it is okay not to like them. If they are far enough removed from us, it is often even recommended that we hate them.

Intelligence officers are occasionally criticized for what some people view as a tendency to identify with the enemy. I have conducted briefings where commanders have disagreed with my assessments because they felt that I was "sympathizing" with the bad guys. Countless times I have had to explain to people that in order to predict what someone is going to do, you need to understand them. Studying hundreds of years of history and oppression does not mean that you agree with their decision to blow up innocent people in a mosque. It means that, hopefully, your understanding will allow you to predict their actions and prevent the innocent people from getting blown up.

For othering to be a thing implies that there is a potential for the opposite. Selfing.

If we like ourselves, then we dislike "others", but if we dislike ourselves then the "selfs" are the ones that we are suspicious of.

There are a lot of ideas of what is of value that are presented to us as we grow and develop, and consciously or not, they impact us. We can agree or disagree with them, but we cannot avoid them.

So, I think that the self that I was when I began my military career was already questioning its value, and then the career I embarked upon spent its time studying those things that were not like me. When I eventually gained more experience and education to better understand the flaws in many of my developmental foundations, I had already begun to create flaws that the more mature me determined had decreased my value.

The end result was that for me, if I viewed my "self" as flawed then when I "selfed" people I was going to have less patience and be more judgmental of them. If I "othered" people, I was more likely to extend empathy to them and give them the benefit of the doubt.

Animals are not even people, so I place them at the extreme end of the "other" spectrum, which means that I usually give them the grace of time and effort. I am aware that telling them that I don't want to hurt them is not something that they are going to immediately understand so I commit to putting in the effort. With people, I do not have the patience. If I say, "Let's hang out," or if I ask you if you want play mancala, what I mean is "Let's hang out," or "let's play mancala" and if someone wants to start analyzing what I said or what my intent was then I just don't have time for them.

Conversely, my expectations are lower because I have spent too much time seeing people at their worst. If an animal attacks another animal or kills another animal, I can accept that there is a reason for it. There is little room for them to become more than what they are.

People, however, have almost limitless potential and so when they disappoint, the impact of their disappointment is similarly limitless.

When an animal kills another animal, it is because they needed a resource and the other animal either was that resource or was a competitor for that resource. They never kill another animal because they read somewhere that the other animal was bad. They never kill another animal because it believes in a different social structure or because it wears the wrong color of clothes. They never kill another animal because of a religious conviction or a state ideology.

People have no such resource restriction and yet their reasons for killing are almost as limitless as is their potential for good. Their reasons for hate are beyond even a cat's ability to ponder.

I avoided No Tail because he presented a dilemma for me. He was an animal, so he was clearly other, but there was something in him that I recognized as self. I did not want to be confused. There was too much grey. Give me a kitten that has no concept of hate or suffering. Something that still smells innocent. Not something that smells like me.

Ultimately, one of the reasons that I connected with No Tail was because he transcended the human and the animal expectations. Animals are what they are and have little room to become more than what they are. Humans have unlimited ability to become more than what they are but rarely ever do.

No Tail became.

He transcended expectations. He was wholly animal but somehow became more than human.

But I'm getting ahead of myself, because in those early days, I didn't trust, and No Tail had no interest in transcending anything. We were both content to glower from a distance and give each other the silent treatment.

No Tail and I Become Friends

"Sometimes the impossible still feels impossible even after it happens."

REBECCA, FROM "CORPSE POSE", BY THAD KRASNESKY

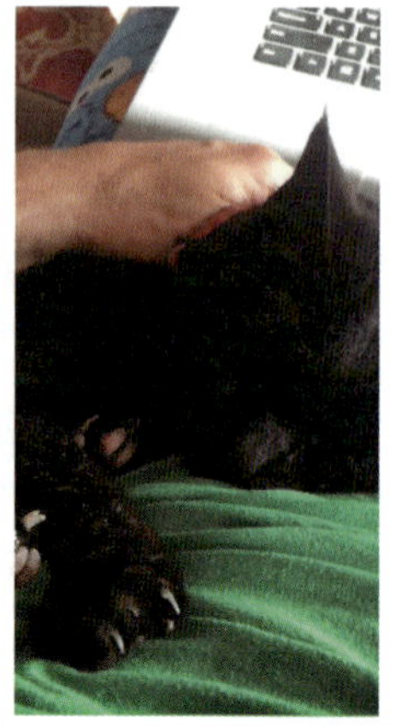

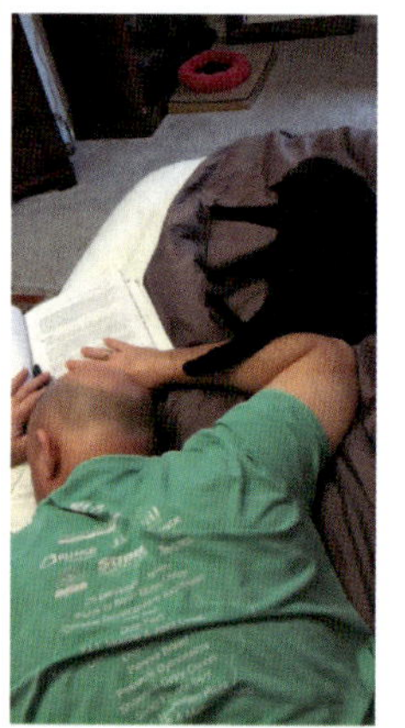
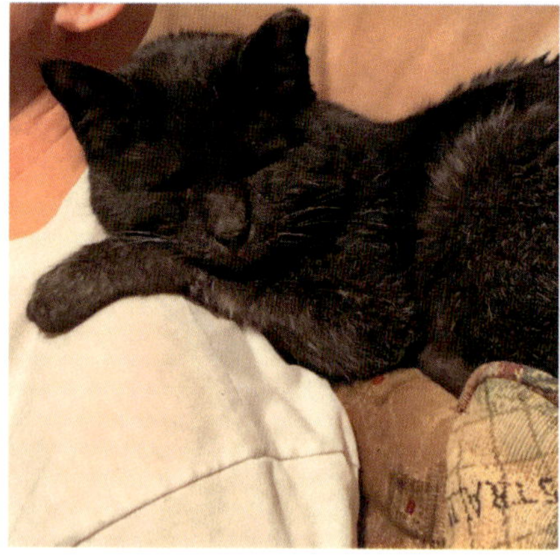

I

No Tail and I did not speak to each other again for almost three weeks.

We began to see each other more frequently though. Usually, every couple of days at the intelligence center, our paths would cross, but it was the early morning runs when no one else was around, where we first began to talk.

I had always been a runner. I ran track in high school and later in the Army, and I had even dreamed of competing in the Olympics at one point, but I lacked the commitment necessary to stay engaged and ignore life's obstacles and distractions. As my PTSD issues became worse however, I had gotten addicted to running, and had begun to participate in ultra-running. The noise and the chaos in my head were so loud and insistent most of the time, but after running for an hour or two the sounds would start to fade, and eventually there would come a point where the only thing I could think about was the next step and the next breath. There was no space for noise, only breathing.

It did not matter what else was going on, I always found time to run. In 2009, I even ran what I believe was the first charity ultra-marathon in a combat zone. I needed a qualifying time within a twelve month period to compete in a hundred mile race when I returned home from that deployment, so I got permission from the race organizers to submit a time from a deployed run if I had other officers there that would swear to my completion of the race and verify the time and distance. I completed the fifty miles in under ten hours and raised a few thousand dollars for Wounded Warrior and Vermont Adaptive while I was at it.

So, with that same commitment that every addict has, I was up at five, six days a week, and running laps around the base in Afghanistan. Occasionally I would see No Tail in the mornings, before I began my runs. I would stretch at the picnic table outside our quarters, and he would be lounging at the feeding station, about halfway down the commons area. I think he liked the predictability. It was not long before he was there every morning.

I would watch him saunter around as I warmed up and stretched, and then afterwards as I cooled down and stretched, and there was nothing in his stride or his stance that would indicate his previous injuries. If you were to get close enough, and were really paying attention, you would notice the unnatural bend at the end of his paw, but few people got that close, and fewer still know how to pay attention. I wouldn't have noticed it myself had I not read his file and looked for it.

It was difficult to know his background and not look down at my own leg as I stretched in the morning and wonder how he had survived.

I could imagine the scenario. I have seen all manner of injured animals, so it was easy to recreate the image in my mind, and I can't help cringing at the thought of an animal with two broken legs just lying there. I want to know what thoughts went through his head in those dark moments.

Did he want to die? Did he want to live? Or did he simply not understand how to not go on?

I think it was probably this last one. I may be projecting a little because we were so much alike, but I suspect that survival was not a conscious choice. It is just a thing that we do. We don't know how not to. We're not brave. We don't have this well of determination that we tap into. We're not overcomers. We simply don't know any better. We lack the ability to view non-continuance as an option. We endure because we are victims of our own pre-determination.

Do humans have free will? Do cats? I don't know. Whatever No Tail and I were at the time, we exercised free will frequently except in the matter of our own existence. Something in our makeup had taken that choice away from us.

Whatever the cause was, No Tail had not had the luxury of simply lying there until his legs healed. There was no one to bring him food. Somehow, he found a way. Somehow, he used those broken legs to not only move, but move enough to find food. And in time he healed.

When I was stationed in California many years ago, we were playing paint ball as a team-building exercise one morning. Near the end of the games, I was running down a hill and my foot caught between two branches that had been covered in leaves. I fell and when I rolled to a stop at the bottom of the hill, my foot was on fire, but the game was still going on, so I got up and kept running.

We played for another thirty minutes before our time was up, and then it was back in the car and back to the barracks.

I did not take my boot off until I got back to my room because I could tell it was already swelling and I didn't want to take it off and then not be able to get it back on. When we did get back to the barracks and I took my boot off, my ankle was black and swollen and hurt like hell. I should have gone immediately to the emergency room. The problem was though that I had a date that evening. I did not want to wind up spending the day in the hospital or have my evening ruined by having my foot in a brace. I figured I could handle it for one day and then if it still felt that bad in the morning, I would go to the hospital.

The date was one of those informal military training base kind of dates. Which meant that we were having pizza and watching a movie in the day room. Basically, the same thing that we had done the previous weekend, but this time it had a label on it, and labels carry consequences. Also, her parents were coming into town that weekend and I was going to have lunch with her entire family at the mess hall.

Lunch came and went. I was limping, but I got through it. Then came the date part. My room was on the third floor. The day room was on the ground floor. At some point in the date, I had to run up to my room for something. And by run, I mean drag myself up one step at a time.

There might have been a book or some cd or something that I was loaning her as well, and then by the end of the evening, she wanted a soda and I had soda in the refrigerator in my room, so I began my third trip up the stairs. By now I was pretty sure my foot was broken. Initially I had thought it had just been sprained, but the swelling and the pain had not gotten any better.

On trip number three, one of my friends saw me sitting on the stairs and pushing myself up backwards, on one foot, one step at a time. They correctly ascertained that this was not normal. After a brief discussion and after coming back down the stairs and limping to the day room to explain things to my date, I climbed into my friend's car and headed to the hospital.

The ER doctor that I saw was concerned at first, but when I told him that I had injured it early that morning, he became more dismissive.

"There's no way that it is broken then. You couldn't have been getting around on it all day if it was broken. It's definitely sprained, but as long as you keep it elevated and put ice on it, it should be fine," was his response.

I had broken bones before and was pretty sure that I had broken my ankle, but what did I know. The ER doctor told me to go back to the barracks and keep it elevated to bring down the swelling. He gave me an athletic bandage to wrap it and told me to go easy on it for the next week. I shrugged and did as he said.

The following morning, my ankle was the size of a large cantaloupe and the color of a ripe eggplant. With a lot of grimacing, and a fair amount of self-righteousness, I returned to the emergency room. There was a different doctor on call at the time who took one look at my ankle and diagnosed it as broken. He sent me to get x-rays immediately and then, unbeknownst to me, called one of the hospital supervisors. When the x-rays were complete and it was determined that I absolutely had broken my ankle the previous day, the supervising doctor asked me to relate to him what had happened the previous evening. He was incredulous at first, but after he fully understood what had transpired, he called in the emergency room doctor from the previous evening and had a professional development discussion with him.

The point is that the ER doctor was insistent that I couldn't have a broken ankle because it simply was not possible for someone to walk around on a broken ankle all day, but what we can endure is often less a matter of physical ability and more a matter of emotional ability and motivation. And in some cases, it is simple ignorance. Not knowing that we can or should just stop.

This is what I thought about as I stretched before heading out on my run, and as I watched the cat with the imperceptible injuries. Neither of us should have been there, but we both lacked the sense to just quit. And perhaps exhibiting that same lack of common sense, I began to talk to No Tail as I stretched, and No Tail, with the same lack of common sense, began to lounge closer and closer to the picnic table each morning.

Perhaps we didn't have free will, because despite our best efforts, we began to become friends.

11

For all of my patience, and years of experience with stray animals, it was tuna that finally sealed the deal. No Tail was getting closer to me each morning, and eventually came within arm's reach, but when I would stretch out to pet him, he would shy away. I enjoyed the companionship and the bond that we were developing, but I wanted to be able to pet him. I needed a physical connection, but I also needed the reassurance of being trusted by an animal.

There were people on the base that he allowed to pet him. He was generally more tolerant of women. The woman who had first recognized him upon his return was one of those persons that cycled through the base every couple of years. She happened to be there in 2015, and although No Tail was far from friendly, with patience and slow movements, she could usually manage to pet him. There were others that he would tolerate, but with me, it always just an arm's reach away.

One evening about a month into my time in Kabul, I was eating dinner at the mess hall when a plan occurred to me. Not so much a plan really. More of an idea. A nebulous and poorly constructed impulse if I'm being honest.

The mess hall had a salad bar, and the salad bar had tuna. Tuna was what had been in the trap when I had first caught No Tail. So, I grabbed a plastic cereal bowl and filled it up with tuna before leaving the mess hall.

The information that I used make my decision to take a bowl of tuna was accurate, but I had not used other information that was also available to me at the time. Like the fact that it was night time and my plan was to give No Tail the tuna while I stretched, which would not occur for another ten hours. Upon returning to my barracks, I reluctantly tucked the bowl of tuna behind the pallet of water bottles, knowing that it would be gone in the morning.

The following evening, I had developed a plan that was only slightly better than my initial one. I once again scooped up a bowl of tuna from the salad bar, but this time I was prepared. I had a plastic bag with me. I was aware that this was not a perfect solution, but as I tucked the bagged up bowl of tuna into my wall locker, I thought, how bad could it really be in just ten hours?

In case you were wondering, it is not particularly warm in Kabul toward the end of April, but it is warm enough that if you keep a bag of tuna in your locker overnight, your roommate is going to notice. After putting on my shorts and shoes the following morning, I opened my locker to retrieve my tuna stash. The aroma did not waft out as much as it marched out clumsily and stumbled over all of the air in the room, punching and kicking as it went. As I hurriedly left the room, my roommate began making sounds that indicated he was either waking up from a bad dream, or possibly choking to death. I wasn't certain which and chose not to stick around to find out.

The positive take away from this though was that the odor of tuna was not subtle as I came to the bottom of the stairs and spilled out the contents of the bag at the foot of the picnic table. No Tail was as subtle as the smell of fish as he stood up and stared at me.

"So," he seemed to be saying. "You think just because you waltz in here with tuna that I'm going to rush over and be your friend now just to get to the fish? You know, I could just kill you and eat you AND the tuna."

Rarely have I seen an animal so conflicted, but he was not going to give in that easily. As I continued to stretch, waiting for him to succumb to the desire for fish, he did the exact opposite. He composed himself, and then settled back down and closed his eyes, as if he could not care less whether or not I had fish at my feet.

I didn't have time to just stand there and wait. I had to run. An hour later, when I returned to my picnic bench, the tuna was gone, and there was a smile on No Tail's face, but he did not come any closer to me that day.

Since I needed something shelf-stable, and less aromatic, I accessed the supply area later that day and borrowed some canned tuna. The following morning, as soon as I stepped over to the picnic table, I popped open the can of tuna and scooped it out into a fresh bowl for No Tail.

It took three days for No Tail to finally approach me and eat the tuna while I was standing there. It took another week before he allowed me to pet him while he ate. It took about two weeks for No Tail to determine that this was now his new routine, which is when his craving for tuna suddenly became the entire barracks problem.

No Tail was big on accountability, and once he had decided that I had contractually agreed to source tuna for him every morning, he was going to hold me to that contract. Loudly and publicly.

Now the base might have rescinded the order to kill stray animals several years previously, but it had not rescinded the order restricting people from feeding the animals. Approved people were allowed to offer them approved food at approved feeding stations, but you were absolutely not allowed to feed them outside of those parameters.

There were plenty of people that violated that order. Most people knew to be discrete about it though. And although I had not intended to make the issue public, No Tail had yet to grasp the concept of discreet. The first morning that I was just a few minutes late getting on my running gear and heading downstairs, the most godawful shouting began out on the commons area. It was that part animal, part air raid siren, part eldritch terror from the abyss sound that I had hear a month before. In my heart, I knew immediately what it was, but my mind told me that there was no way possible that a twelve-pound cat could make a sound like that.

I rushed down the stairs as quickly as I could and as soon as I stepped out of the door, the sounds stopped. It was replaced by the politest meow possible. I stared at the cat in front of me trying to fathom how such a sound could have come out of such a small being. No Tail looked at me so innocently that on that first morning I had almost convinced myself that there had to have been another animal out there, maybe a sabertoothed tiger or something, that had made that hideous noise. There was no way that it could have come from him.

A week later, the truth was confirmed. I am not even certain that I was running late this time, but perhaps he was just early. Regardless of the reason, the sounds of supernovas shrieking in the galactic mosh pit once more filled the pre-dawn realm of those who still wanted to be asleep. This time I made the mistake of looking out the window before running down the stairs. I didn't want to be gaslighted again and have the howling stop the moment I stepped out of the door on the ground floor.

In the still-dark morning, there was enough illumination from the security lights for No Tail to see a head stick out of the window and for him to recognize me. As soon as he saw me, he stopped yelling, but the damage was done. He knew which room was mine.

I pulled my head back in the window and headed downstairs. As soon as I stepped away from the window, the howling started again. And once again, as soon as I stepped outside, it stopped, but not before several other windows had been thrown open to see if the alien attack had finally begun.

That became the norm. As long as I was down the stairs before five fifteen, all was well, but if I missed it by a minute, alarms would go off and there would be a small black cat pacing on the ground beneath my third-floor window.

We quickly settled into a routine. Every day would start with five minutes of stretching and petting, an hour of running, and then another ten minutes of stretching and petting. It was a comfortable routine to fall into, but it was also a troubled one. I realized that I was once again forming a bond with an animal that I would have to leave behind. One more abandonment. One more broken promise. One more piece of myself left behind, and I did not have many pieces left.

I wondered though, how many pieces did No Tail have left? I had befriended a dozen different animals across my five deployments and had had to leave every single one of them, but how many people had come into and gone out of No Tail's life over the seven years that he had been alive? A dozen? Two dozen? A hundred?

How many times had he allowed someone to get close to him and touch him and show him love, only to have them vanish? I was hesitant to bond with him because of a dozen separations in my past. How much more hesitant must he have been to have gone through that time after time after time. I knew that I was setting myself up to have my heart broken again, but the worst part for me each time was not the loss itself. It was not being able to explain to the animal that I had befriended that I wasn't abandoning them out of choice. And I didn't want to bond with No Tail and become his friend because I didn't want to return to the states at the end of my deployment and wonder if No Tail was still wandering around looking for me. Showing up at our picnic bench and wondering when I was going to come back.

But like most bad choices, that was a pain that I would deal with tomorrow. Right now, this was all that I had. With reservations on both sides, we accepted our new routine.

And that is how our friendship began. It was definitely transactional, and it took a long time for it to transition into something more. Unfortunately, as our relationship developed, my emotional state deteriorated.

III

For No Tail, routine soon became sacrosanct. It was an immutable truth that I would show up every day between five and five fifteen. Unfortunately, no one had explained Sundays to No Tail.

As obsessively as I run, I still know that rest days must be taken. For me, rest days were Sundays. I am sure at some point in my hyper-religious past, this was part of my act of faith, but over the course of the last few deployments, God and I had had a falling out. We still talked occasionally but it often became contentious. Sure, it would start out cordially enough. I would ask him how he was doing and if he had made any really cool sunsets recently, and he would ask me how my writing was coming along, but then eventually I would make some comment about starving children in a joking manner but he would see through the humorous veneer, because, you know, he's God, and he would realize that it wasn't a joke but was really a judgmental comment directed at him, and he would respond with some cutting remark about the sixth commandment, and then I would point out that it was his fault for creating us in the first place and then I would probably go off topic and make some crack about what kind of idiot would create mosquitoes, and once it got personal like that we would both start raising our voices, and then you knew the night was going to end with both of us giving the other the cold shoulder.

So mostly I took Sundays off because you can't run every day and expect your body to recover.

I do not know what No Tail's relationship with God was at that point in his life, but he was definitely not a fan of Sundays, and he had no tolerance for day's off. I discovered this after we were about three weeks into our new morning routine. He had been an occasional morning visitor when I had first began my runs, but after tuna was introduced and we broke that initial contact barrier, he started showing up every morning, whether there was tuna or not. And if he was going to show up, then his expectation was that I show up as well.

It was five fifteen on Sunday morning, and since it was a Sunday, it is probably appropriate to call the sound that arose from the common's area outside the barracks as an unholy howl. Amid muffled curses and shouts of "Go feed your cat!", I rushed downstairs as quickly as possible.

As usual, as soon as I stepped outside, he ceased his meowing and walked over to the picnic table and sat down in our spot. It was five fifteen, and since I wasn't planning on running that day, my next hour was free. Thus began our new routine of Sunday pets.

It was also during these morning sessions that I began to understand No Tail's relationship with other cats. The many cats on base all had their own personalities. Some hung out in small groups, others hung out with another cat as a bonded pair. There were a few that interacted peacefully with many different cats but didn't have a particular group they belonged to. A few of them were more solitary in nature, like No Tail. In general, his approach was to not approach other cats. He avoided them when he could and ignored them when he could not. There was a feeding station near our barracks and I think that the reason that No Tail was in that area in the morning in the first place was because it allowed him an opportunity to eat in peace, when it was less likely that other cats would be around. Basically, the same reason that I ran at that time of day.

He had aggression issues from the first time that I met him. He did not generally seek fights with other cats, because he didn't seek other cats, but if there was a cat anywhere nearby that looked at him the wrong way or smelled like it was up to no good or had bad taste in music, or whatever other random criteria he used to judge the other cats, he would make them leave or at the very least he would make them avert their eyes and apologize for their offense. In other words, he rarely started fights himself, but he was always on the lookout for a cat that was ready to start something.

I saw him in minor scuffles several times. Twice, I saw him engage in actual fights, and one was a battle royale of epic proportions.

Across the base was a garden area where units would hold events and cook outs. There were a few cats in that area, but the undisputed king was a giant of a feline called Monster. Monster was half cat, half tyrannosaurs rex. He weighed over twenty five pounds, and he had long hair so he looked even bigger. I knew

Monster from my work with the FCC, but I had never seen him outside of his Kingdom of the Barbecue Pits.

I don't know why he came over to the barracks that morning, but No Tail sensed him before I even knew he was there. It seemed possible to me that Monster might have come over just to fight with No Tail, because there was no delay in his movements. No Tail looked up, I looked up to where No Tail was looking, and around the corner came Monster, charging straight at us and breathing fire. No Tail was on his feet and racing toward Monster before I could even think about reacting. When they collided, you could feel the impact through the ground.

I do not recommend ever being in a position where you witness a monolithic cat fight like that. This is not the play fighting of domestic cats, or even the angry territorial fighting of strays. This was gladiator in the colosseum kind of thing where annihilation of your opponent is your only goal. I was immediately afraid for No Tail's life because it did not seem likely that he would have any chance of defeating the massive cat that was twice his size, but my first reaction was to stand in awe and watch. It was violence, but it was compelling violence, like watching a tornado, and I found it hard to look away.

Reason finally broke through my awe, and I knew that I had to try to break it up. If I had had my uniform on, I might have been able to throw the thick jacket over one of the cats to separate them, but all I had on was my t-shirt, and it would do nothing to stop the carnage. There was a trash can not far away and I considered trying to lower it down on top of one of them, but the odds on that seemed pretty low as well. I did not want to leave the area to find better equipment or look for help, so finally I settled on my best course of action being to grab a bottle of water from the water pallet and try to separate them by dousing them with water.

By the time I grabbed the water though, it was already over. No Tail and Monster had merged into a tangled ball of hissing fur, but then I saw No Tail grab the larger cat in his mouth and literally throw him. Before Monster could get his bearings, No Tail leapt onto him again and kicked him with his back feet so hard that it raised dust when the other cat landed yet again.

No Tail turned to look at me, and I don't know if Monster viewed this as the beginning of a retreat from No Tail which would give him an opportunity for a new attack, but whatever his thoughts were, they were mistaken. As he leapt toward No Tail again, No Tail sprung up and all but levitated so that

Monster grabbed nothing but air. Monster quickly realized his mistake and tried to disengage, but there was a switch that had been flipped inside No Tail, and he was not going to relent. When I finally got the cap off the bottle and slung the water over the two combatants, it was Monster and not No Tail that I was now trying to save. The shock of the water caused them to disengage, and Monster wasted no time in fleeing from the area. No Tail just turned and looked at me.

I have seen people with murder in their eyes before. Many, many times. I saw that look in No Tail's face that day and recognized it for what it was. He was filled with rage, and completely untethered from reason. Even if he and I had been friends at that point, I don't think I would have approached him. I'm not sure he would have been able to discern friend from foe. There was nothing left behind those eyes but anger, and if it is possible for an animal to hate, there was hate there as well.

He looked around for some target to direct his rage onto. I almost thought for a moment that he might even attack me, but he did not. When he finally completed his scan of the area and was frustrated in his search for someone to attack and vent his rage upon, he looked at me again, and then walked away. He did not return for several days, and I pushed my runs harder than usual the next few mornings, as if I could somehow burn off his anger with my own exertions.

When he finally did return, he communicated that he didn't wish to talk about the fight. We did not. But I did hang around longer that day to pet him and to tell him that it was okay.

IV

I had bitten into this final deployment of mine, with my mouth already full of the bitter aftertaste of expectations that were past their expiration dates. I had stopped paying my mental electric bill so any chicken soup for my soul that was still sitting in the refrigerator that had hummed to a halt about three deployments ago was now starting to grow mold on the humid surface of its congealed grease. Everything left inside me had gone off.

It was my intention to harden myself and shut down all but the necessary functions to get through the months ahead. I would deal with whatever was left when I returned.

As Burns once did not quite say though, no matter how well the mice or the man lays his plans, when a cat enters the picture, thing are about to get ganged well and truly aglee.

Developing a relationship with No Tail was effectively punching holes in the armor I was trying to put on. It wasn't just animals, either. I also found that my guard was lowered when it came to people as well. The team that I worked with made it harder for me to stay isolated by being decent people.

It is both easy and accurate to make the statement "I don't know what would have happened if…" Our lives are filled with those moments. We usually don't recognize them because most people's days are not filled with monumental and easily identifiable repercussions.

We don't know what would have happened if we had taken one job instead of another. We don't know what would have happened if we dated this person instead of that person. We don't know what would have happened if we had taken this road to work this morning instead of that one, or what would have happened if we had put lettuce on our sandwich instead of just tomatoes.

I don't know what would have happened if I had not had No Tail with me at that point in my life. That is true. But to say that only vaguely implies why it is relevant and since this book is an attempt to be as authentic and open as possible, I will say what that vague observation implies.

I struggle making friends. I don't think that I am easy to be friends with. If my friendship came with a warning label like certain toys or games do, it would say "Recommended for advanced friendship building audiences only. Not a beginner model."

Developmentally, I missed a lot of opportunities to create normal social patterns and friendships. Bandura or Gesell might say that I will remain a puzzled six-year-old until I find a way to process my trauma. Denisovich would counter that, as long as I have a piece of cheese and bread, moral age is more important than mental age. And Poklemba would point out that a tendency to refer to Bandura or Denisovich in casual conversation makes me sound like a pretentious git and is probably a big part of my problem.

Regardless of which one is right, I also have the experiential issues to deal with that have created irrational fears that I hold in mutual contradiction to what I know. I have shared with my wife that there are times I feel like the life I have lived and the things I have done have created an odor around me. A pheromone that I exude that smells like death. I know that it is not true while at the same time fearing that it is. I feel at times like this weird, M. Night Shyamalan, incongruous, death-scented child thing that walks around haunting myself and cursed to always ask why but never knowing the answer.

You can see how that might be an impediment to a desire to engage socially.

In the past, my combat relationships were built on action. I worked with a small team of people, and we spent all of our time doing stuff, which is very bonding, but it does not leave a lot of room for thinking and getting to know each other. In the role I was assigned to in Kabul, I was in charge of a team of people working in an office. There was very little action. There was a lot of talking.

We listened to music. We watched shows. We played sports. We were people who happened to be soldiers instead of soldiers who were occasionally allowed to be some faint reflection of people.

No Tail made me work for his friendship, and so I was already engaging social muscles that I rarely used. It made me emotionally sore and gave me relationship tendonitis, but it better prepared me to use those same muscles to become friends with the people with which I worked.

I'm not saying that I was a good friend. Expecting me to be a good friend would be like expecting someone who hasn't played basketball in twenty years to be able to go out on the court and sink their first free-throw. But I was at least trying. I was out on the court. Dropping the ball and tripping over myself most of the time, but I was at least playing. It was a very lonely time in my head during those months in Kabul, and if I had been truly alone, I could have seen a scenario where I just became one of those people that walked off a base and never returned. More likely, I would have done something that would have landed me in jail, or at the very least, kicked out of the Army.

It also helped that my team had a little bit of other about them to begin with. I don't mean their countries of origin, although that helped. I mean that they all felt the challenge of being placed in a less than ideal position but were expected to contribute to ideal results. They even adopted a mascot and a motto. The mascot was a honey badger, as in "honey badger don't care" to indicate that we were able to put up with whatever circumstances were sent our way. Their motto was "Materiam superabat opus." Literally it means, "the workmanship exceeds the material." Colloquially, they more commonly quoted it to mean, "give us shit to work with and we'll still find a way to make something productive."

As someone who had once been a member of "The Chocolate Milkmen" and "Team Shepherd", I wore my Honey Badger unit patch on my shoulder proudly, even though it was not exactly authorized. Their non-standard personalities and professional attitudes were a good bridge for me.

And in a slight, but not complete, departure from the topic at hand, I want to share one of my favorite anecdotes about the honey badger team. Since we were an international team, some of our members had distinct phrases or terms that they would use. Our Australian captain occasionally used the word "whilst."

Whilst is a perfectly acceptable word. A great word even. But since some senior American officer felt like the word was too Britishy, even though, if he had bothered to check, he would have discovered that we were in fact allies with the British, we were advised not to use "whilst" in our reports.

We took offense at that, so we made a game out of it. There is a popular comedy sketch out there that uses the phrases "insubordinate and churlish" and "mischievous and deceitful" among others. The game was to see if we could slip one of those phrases into a briefing. Quite possibly one of my proudest moments in my military career was when one of our officers, with a straight face, briefed that the Taliban was engaging in tactics that were both "chicanerous and deplorable."

But even with my growing connection to No Tail, and the tenuous but real connections to other people that he helped me make, our true nature is hard to subdue for long. The death-scented child with his persistent "Why" would soon make an appearance.

V

As the chief for CJIOC-NATO, I was occasionally included in some of the more performative dog-and-pony show briefings that were given to visiting dignitaries and politicians. Usually, I was nothing more than a back-bencher, but there were times that they wanted to hang bells on my reins and see how well I could prance.

Prior to one of these briefings, it had been made clear to us that a senior individual from the state department was interested in hearing reports that would support a position that they were trying to advance. The position was bollocks, of course, and the truth did not support it, so when I was asked to brief my three bullet points, I made sure that they clearly communicated my analysis that what was being proposed was a poor choice.

It was obvious to everyone that my comments were intentionally confrontational. I was still looking for that hill to die on, and I figured if I could piss off some bureaucratic wonk along the way, all the better.

It did not piss him off though. It amused him, and he asked me to stay behind for a few moments after the briefing. I thought, aha, here it is. He kept his calm during the public meeting, but I must have gotten to him and now the verbal beatings will commence.

His smile only got wider after everyone left though. He told me that he appreciated my honesty and asked me what I was trying to accomplish with my comments. I told him that all I wanted to accomplish was the truth. He actually laughed as he told me that what I had said in the briefing was irrelevant, because the truth was going to be whatever they told people it was.

It wasn't the injustice of what he said that got to me. It was the smugness with which he said it that stuck with me. The gloating certainty that he was in control and that there was nothing that anyone could do about it.

I witnessed that same look on the face of a terrorist once, when he had smiled gleefully at the fear he had created in a small child. I have seen evil more times than I care to recall, but when I think about evil, it is the image of that smug smile that comes to my mind as often as any of the more gruesome images. The sick need to make the innocent tremble for no purpose other than to remind them that they were powerless. The obscene level of self-assurance that he was in control and that there was nothing that could be done about it. He found out later that he was mistaken, but that conclusion did nothing to stem the tide of glee that evil luxuriates in when the powerful make the innocent suffer.

It is one thing to see that look on the face of an enemy combatant, but quite another to see it on the face of a representative from your own government. I was not even reprimanded for my transgression. It was more satisfying for him to know that reminding me of my powerlessness was punishment enough.

I was already several months into the deployment at this time, but the end seemed impossibly far away. This experience deepened the emptiness and the helplessness that I felt inside, and I knew that if I did not find some way to feel like I was making a difference soon, I would start to shut down. I had already had every suggestion that I had made get denied though.

I talked to No Tail about this during one of our Sunday morning non-running days. His suggestions were not helpful. I did not think that biting the state department representative would have accomplished anything, and that was the least violent of his suggestions. He told me that if I was going to ignore his ideas just because they involved biting people, then he wasn't sure that he was willing to help, but that if I would bring some more tuna, he would think on it.

Revisiting the incident with No Tail got me spun up and I was starting to consider his biting suggestion, I decided to go running instead, even though it was a rest day. That keyed an idea for me. Running helped relieve my stress. I understood the chemistry behind it and knew that this was not a unique reaction. Most people had similar experiences when they ran. So, what if I organized a run like I had in Salman Pak, but did it for the entire base instead of just for myself? They could hardly argue that physical fitness was not supporting the mission.

With hesitant optimism, I pitched the idea of organizing a marathon for the base. It had fitness, esprit de corps, and just a sprinkle of senseless machismo to it, which turned out to be the perfect recipe to have the project approved. Finally, something that was in my wheelhouse that I could sink my teeth into.

No Tail appreciated the metaphor when I told him about it, but he was still in favor of biting someone in a non-metaphorical manner.

I measured several different route options with GPS and engineering tools. There were no clear routes that could be properly connected with streets on the base so any route that was selected was going to have to take some creative approaches. I didn't want to wind up running a hundred laps on the quarter mile loop of road around the motor pool, but I also didn't want to create a route that required "shinny through the access alley behind the mess hall, making sure to avoid the protruding pipes, then leap over the hedges at the opposite end and turn right" to be part of the directions. After trying about a dozen different options, I finally came up with one that required relatively few laps, limited road closures, and only one choke point where runners would have to thread a corner between one of the buildings and a security wall.

No Tail was instrumental during each step of the process. It required a lot more running than I was used to, so I started getting up even earlier to log the necessary miles and test each new route. The first morning I got up at four thirty instead of five to start my run. As I came around the back side of the first lap, I heard that familiar howl again. No Tail had not been there when I had started my run that morning, so when I did not appear at our normally scheduled time, he assumed that I was rudely sleeping in and ignoring him. I had to take a detour from my planned route and come over to the picnic table to reassure him that I was already up. He was not happy about it, but he at least stopped howling.

The day that I ran a test marathon on the route, he was even less pleased. He tolerated my even earlier start that morning, but after I kept going around and around, without showing any sign of stopping, he began to get agitated. He would normally lay there patiently while I completed my morning runs, but as my run extended more than an hour past my usual end time, he began to stand up every time I turned the corner and came into view. By the end of the next hour, he began to pace impatiently, and toward the end of the run he began to call out to me as I passed. Not a full-throated howl, which might have necessitated my ending the run, but an incessant inquiry as if he was concerned that something had gone wrong.

Everything was coming along nicely, and I had even begun to print out flyers and set out signup sheets. Then I made the fatal error of turning the run into a fundraiser for charity. I thought that since the run was already approved, we might as well step it up a notch and have an even greater impact.

I was never given a specific reason for why the run was canceled. The charity part was never mentioned. Just a lot of vague statements about it being a distraction to mission accomplishment, but never an explanation as to why that would be.

As soon as my shift was over on the day that I received notice that the marathon had been canceled, I went back to my room and changed into my running clothes. Someone was going to run that marathon, and it didn't matter what time it was. I ran angry, which was nothing new, but this time I found it hard to find that peace that running usually brings me. When I was finished, it was almost two in the morning, and I went over to the picnic table to stretch.

Sitting there, in our usual spot, was No Tail.

I rarely saw him around the barracks in the evening, and I had no idea what hidden den on the base he actually called home, but there he was. He was silent as I approached him. Not even his usual polite meows that he often greeted me with. Just a look of concern on his face that communicated his understanding to me.

"You're angry," it said. "I get it. And I can tell you're going through some things right now so I'm not going to ask questions, but you do know that running a marathon at night is a little weird, right? Okay. As long as you see that. And since you're already up, you can sit here and pet me if you want. I'll be angry right next to you."

When I got to my office later that morning, my team did not need to have the scenting ability of an animal to know that I was upset. Our Finnish officer who was always looking for a reason to hold an impromptu dance party, threw a "Thirty Minute Pop-Up Disco" in the office, complete with colored lights. I still have no idea where he got those. Our small suite of offices was quickly filled with people he had invited over from all of the international groups that we worked with, and for thirty minutes the intelligence center for NATO forces in Afghanistan was turned into a giant mosh pit.

The celebration ended promptly at the thirty minute mark, as advertised. He had determined that anything that lasted longer than an hour risked losing the right to be labeled as a "pop-up" and it also was likely to draw too much negative attention from people who did not appreciate the loud mixture of Swedish disco and Polish metal that was pounding the walls. Our Australian officer broke out his carefully parceled out stash of Tim Tam's after the disco and shared them with everyone, and later in the day, our Estonian captain, who looked like a Viking but was an amazing chess player even let me win a game of chess against him.

I hadn't realized until that moment that I mattered to other people, and I certainly hadn't realized that I mattered enough for them to do something like this for me because they cared that I was upset. It was in this moment of disappointment that I accepted that friendship with people and not just cats, was a choice that was open to me. I would tentatively build upon this moment and develop those friendships further with "Foreign Movie Night" where each one of us would bring a movie from his home country and we would watch it and discuss it afterwards, and "Open Mic Night" where we coopted a stage in one of the recreation buildings and invited people over to sing a song or read poetry or do interpretive dance or however they felt like best expressing themselves in an environment that did not always encourage self-expression, and even "Embassy Runs" where we would bring our entire dusty band through the security turnstiles to invade the greenspace of the adjacent embassy and partake of their juice bar and swim in their pool.

The ripples continue to this day. I have developed friendships with people after returning home that I had served with in Afghanistan but did not really put in the effort to get to know. Had I taken the time, I might have developed some even more wonderful memories, and I regret that I missed out on getting to know so many other people when I had the chance.

But I am still thankful for the friendships that I had, and it was the connection with that angry black cat that allowed me to open up enough to make those other friendships possible.

VI

The friendships, however, were not the happy ending. It would have been great if the story had ended at the disco, with everyone dancing and smiling. Roll credits, turn on the lights, and everyone go home happy.

There were two large impediments to that being the happy ending. One was the fact that there was actually a war still going on. It's hard to live happily ever after when a lot of people wouldn't even get to experience the "live" part for very long. The second problem was that I was still filled with rage. The runs had not exercised it. The dance had not cured it. The friendships did not heal it. And rage is like fire. If it isn't extinguished, it will find a way to blaze up again. All it needs is food.

In August, the Taliban began a major offensive across the country. In Kabul, they killed over fifty people in a series of bomb attacks. One of those even hit the Special Operations base that I was originally supposed to be assigned to.

In southern Afghanistan, two Special Forces soldiers were killed as the Taliban launched a massive attack on the district capital in Musa Qalah and seized it from the government forces. The following day I was part of a briefing to a senior officer about the situation, where we had informed him that the Taliban was now in control of the district and that retaking the district would cost hundreds of lives. The assessment was also provided to him that retaking the district would be a wasted effort because even if it were retaken, there was not enough power to hold it long-term. I was somewhat surprised then when the following day, that same officer issued a press release stating that the US "would not let Musa Qalah fall."

As a follow up, it was pointed out to him that, per the previous briefing, Musa Qalah already HAD fallen. His response was that we would need to retake it then because people had to know that we were going to keep our word.

A reminder was offered that, per the previous briefing, retaking it would cost hundreds of lives. He asked, "Afghanistan or American?"

At which point, it is possible that someone with anger issues might have made an observation along the lines of, "You are putting your ego ahead of the lives of your soldiers."

That is how it possibly might have gone down. Hypothetically.

Regardless of the exact words that were exchanged, within fifteen minutes of me returning to my office, I received a call from my commander informing me that I had been personally selected to be the intelligence officer that would coordinate with the Afghan intelligence personnel in an upcoming operation in southern Afghanistan.

In a little town called Musa Qalah.

I had two hours to pack my bags and be ready at the helicopter landing pad.

For Robin's birthday that year, along with whatever gift I had purchased online and sent to her, she also got a phone call, but it was not the usual cheerful "Happy Birthday" one might expect, or even a somewhat subdued "happy birthday" that is offered during stressful times. It was "Happy Birthday, and oh, by the way, I have to go be part of an operation that I just briefed two days ago is basically a suicide mission."

I left out that last part of course.

Communication is key to any good relationship, and when you are engaged in a profession that requires you to moderate much of your communication it is not a good thing. The call was restrained, and the tone was flat. I told her that I wouldn't be able to call her or email her as frequently over the next few weeks, if at all. I could hear her quiet acceptance on the other end.

Some spouses get cake for their birthday. Some get calls filled with subtext saying that you might not come home.

For a final call, it was brief. I was already packed. This left me with an hour before I had to leave. It wasn't enough time to get a run in so I did the only other thing that I could think of. I went looking for No Tail.

It was late afternoon and locating him at any time other than our standing morning appointment was never certain. It took me half an hour before I finally found him over by the gazebo.

We sat down together, and he put his head on my leg and let me pet him. I tried to explain to him that I would be gone for a little while and that I would come back, but that if I didn't come back, I hadn't left him. I just hadn't been able to return. I told him that I loved him, and I started to cry.

It was not the first time that I had cried while talking to No Tail, and he had never seemed to react to it before but this time he did. This time he bit me.

And I know that this is a book about a cat, and often we have to suspend belief for a moment as we make assumptions about what an animal is thinking or communicating to us, but sometimes the message is so clear that no assumption is necessary, and it doesn't matter that it is an animal that is saying it. We know what we know.

When No Tail bit me, he sat up and stared at me. He stared at me with that look that he had had when he had fought Monster. It wasn't just anger. It was rage. It was hate. Not hate toward me but hate that was a thing existing independent of any need for an object upon which to project it, and I understood what he was telling me.

Now is not the time to be sad. Now is the time to rage. Now is the time to become as dark as you need to be. Cry later, when you come home. But for now, rage.

So I promised him I would. From one dark soul to another, I promised him rage.

And I did.

VII

I was in Musa Qalah for almost a month. When I returned, the first thing that I did was sleep. I had done very little of that in the previous few weeks. Then when I woke up, I ran.

I did not see any sign of a black cat when I stretched, or when I ran, or when I finished my run. I asked around and was told that No Tail had come howling for a few days after I left but then had stopped. I was assured that people had seen him around, but no one could tell me exactly when or where he had last been seen.

I brought tuna with me the next morning when I went running, but still no sign of him. By the end of the day, I was beginning to get nervous, but the following morning my fears were allayed when he casually showed up as if no time had passed. I was glad to see him, but now another concern was beginning to raise its head. My deployment was coming to an end. In three weeks, I would be going home. And then what would become of him?

I had made friendships with animals on every one of my deployments. A litter of puppies on one occasion, two young tuxedo cats on another, a tired, older female dog on one, and even a small flock of magpies. Every time I bonded with them, knowing that I would have to leave.

So here I was again, in the same situation. Getting ready to leave someone else behind. For the first time, I considered the idea of using social media to address the issue. The internet was filled with heartwarming rescue stories, so why not make it happen?

I started a social media page for No Tail, and began posting pictures of him, and quoting observations that he might share with me on the page. My hope was that someone would see him and fall in love with him and find a way to bring him home. It wasn't my intention at that point to take him home to live with me. We already had too many cats, and I did not feel capable of handling the responsibility I already would have upon my return home, let alone taking on the responsibility for another creature. I couldn't just leave him though. I needed to know that he was going to be okay.

It is tediously difficult, however, to create a miracle. His page developed a small following, but no one stepped forward and said, "I'll give him a home and figure out a way to get him here." We had by that time figured out the logistics of it, but the cost to bring an animal to the states from Afghanistan was almost three thousand dollars in 2015, and we simply didn't have the money to do it, even if we had wanted to.

A wiser, calmer black cat would later tell me, "When the miracles don't happen, you have to become the miracle."

A week before I was scheduled to leave, I was in a panic. We had no prospects and no money, and we were quickly running out of options. I was talking to Robin on the phone about it when she just interrupted me and said, "Just get him. We'll figure it out."

Robin is not an impulsive person. She likes plans that have backup plans for the backup plans. She prefers options that have exit strategies. She is deliberate. Probably the three most impulsive things she ever has done in her life is marry me, ask me to buy this big, old mansion for her, and tell me to "just get" this black cat from Afghanistan.

"Just getting him" turned out to be more difficult than anticipated. He pulled another disappearing act on me.

I don't know if he was still not back in his normal routine from the disruption caused by my foray south, or if he smelled something suspicious in the air, but he went AWOL for three days. He had occasionally broken routine and gone missing for a day or two, but three days was unlike him. I was afraid that I had waited too long. What if he had gone on a walkabout and that was just it? Gone. I would never see him again. Or what if something had happened to him? He had gone for a year without any serious injuries, which was a record for him, so what if he had finally gone back to old patterns and was lying somewhere, injured?

I decided that the best thing to do was to go back to what you know. And so, the next day I went to the veterinary care center and got three of the FCC live traps and baited them all with tuna. That evening, an unmistakable howling could be heard from the trap beneath the gazebo. Regardless of what he might or might not suspect, he simply couldn't resist the tuna.

I took him immediately to the care center where we logged him in. I informed the vet that I would be sending him to the clinic run by Now Zad to be vetted for eventual transfer to the states. They asked if I had found a sponsor for him. I told him that I would figure it out. Robin's declaration seemed to be enough for him, and we let Now Zad know that we had a cat heading their way.

The next hurdle was getting a gate pass. Typically, you have to submit a request for a gate pass several days in advance to give the base commander time to review why you need to leave the base and decide whether or not to approve or disapprove it. With the cat center, it was fairly routine, and they were never turned down, but they were always submitted a week in advance.

I did not have a week to wait.

I transferred No Tail to a carrier and headed to the gate. Fortunately, the people at the gate knew me. I did brief walkabouts once a week with a couple of members of my team to conduct liaison operations at the nearby provincial security headquarters, or occasionally at the Afghan army intel center a little bit further down the Bibi Mahru, and any rumors that you might have heard that we were actually going off base because we had found a bakery that made the best naan bread you have ever tasted is absolutely unfounded and purely delicious. I mean, malicious.

Anyway, as I approached the gate, I did not go through the security office and the clearance area, and the access walkway, and then the exit station, where they triple-check to make sure that you have the proper gear and authorizations. Instead, I went around the series of chicanes and directly to the large vehicle gate, with the small postern gate to its side. I was told to stop a couple of times as I approached the gate, and for a moment I thought someone might even draw on me, but since I was leaving the base with two cat carriers in my arms, and not approaching the base with an IED, they were more curious than suspicious.

Two carriers?

Yeah, I'll explain that in a bit, but we're in a hurry.

The guard at the door told me that I needed to stop and turn around and go through the checkpoint. I held up the carriers and said, "I have a cat," and then just stepped around him.

It is a truth in life that is constantly reenforced in the intel world, that if you act like you can do a thing, you are more likely to be allowed to do the thing and less likely to get shot. Robin and I were once in DC and were walking on the National Mall when we decided to visit the Smithsonian. Robin was certain that we would be stopped and that they would not allow us to take Lola, our chihuahua, into the museum.

Initially, she was right. They did stop me. The guard at the metal detectors told me that I was not allowed to bring a dog into the museum.

"No. It's okay, " I told him. "I'm allowed to."

Both the guard and Robin watched me with some confusion as I tucked my dog under my arm and headed inside. Then Robin shrugged and followed me inside.

My disclaimer is that you actually have to be willing to get shot when you try something like this, so I do not recommend it. However, in this case, it worked.

Once outside and standing on the edge of the Bibi Mahru, I looked around for the cab. We had called one before leaving the FCC clinic, but cabs in Kabul are not always reliable and I knew that regardless of how confident and authorized I might have appeared, someone was probably calling the guard mount commander right now. It would not be long before less flustered people would appear and insist that I go back inside. I was ready to take the first cab that presented itself to me, but fortunately almost as soon as I stepped outside, a cab saw my cat carriers and pulled up to me.

"Now Zad?" he said, and I nodded my head and said yes. I speak Arabic, and my Urdu is less than rudimentary, but that was enough. I shoved twenty dollars into the cab driver's hand and said, "Thank you," and then put the carriers in the back of the car. I had only a moment to tell No Tail that everything was going to be okay, before the door was closed and the cab disappeared into traffic.

As I turned back to the gate and headed back onto the base, regardless of what I had just told No Tail, I was far from certain that everything would be okay. I didn't know if No Tail would clear the health requirements. If he did, I still didn't know how we were going to get him home. And more importantly, even if we worked through all of that, I was still far from okay.

The new CJIOC-NATO chief had arrived the day before, so with No Tail now gone, and my replacement running the honey badger intelligence cell, I had little to occupy my mind. Our Finnish officer, always looking for an excuse to throw another pop-up disco threw me a "Farewell to Major K Thirty Minute Pop Up Disco". We made a final run to the embassy juice bar, and then I was on a helicopter to Bagram. The process from Kabul to Bagram to Kuwait to El Paso, and finally back to Kansas and home took ten days.

During that time, I received an email from the wife of my closest remaining friend. He and I had known each other for twenty years. We went through language school together in California and ran on the same track team. We were in each other's wedding parties. My older daughter, Rachael had a crush on him when she was three, and always referred to him as "The Man."

I had lost so many friends over the years that my family had an inside joke about it. Whenever I referred to a friend, my girls would immediately interrupt me and ask, "One of the dead ones, or is this one still alive?"

That's some pretty dark humor genes to grow up with. Not very funny, but very real. You might even call it gritty. Just another reminder that trauma is not a solid. At best it is a gel. It leaks. It gets onto everything. Even your kids.

So, this was one of the few that was still alive, but now suddenly he wasn't. "The Man" was gone.

I was going home. I was out of combat theater now. There was no place to rage. So I ran. And ran, and ran, and ran.

When I got off the plane in Kansas City on October 8th, I weighed one hundred and sixty-five pounds. A loss of twenty pounds from my competition weight. The loss had begun a month earlier when I had gone to Musa Qalah and had continued to accelerate the closer I got to home. Two months later, in December, I would be down to one hundred and thirty-eight pounds and would wind up being admitted to a program for soldiers with severe PTSD who have attempted suicide.

No Tail and I Return to Kansas

The woods are lovely, dark, and deep,

But I have promises to keep,

And miles to go before I sleep,

And miles to go before I sleep.

Robert Frost, **"Stopping by Woods on a Snowy Evening"**

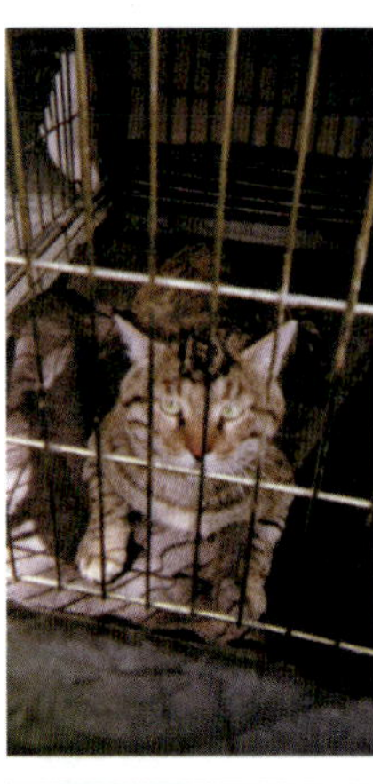

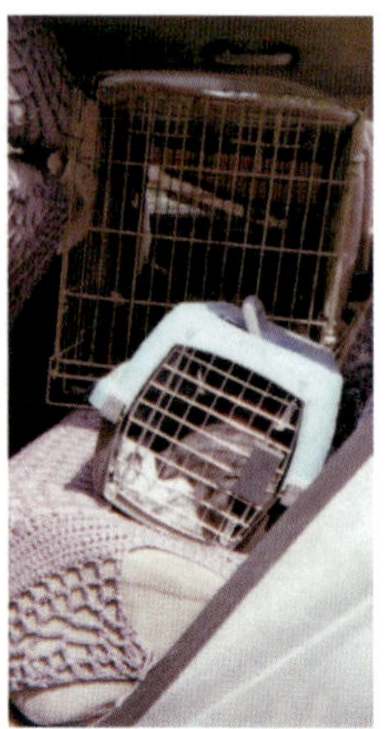
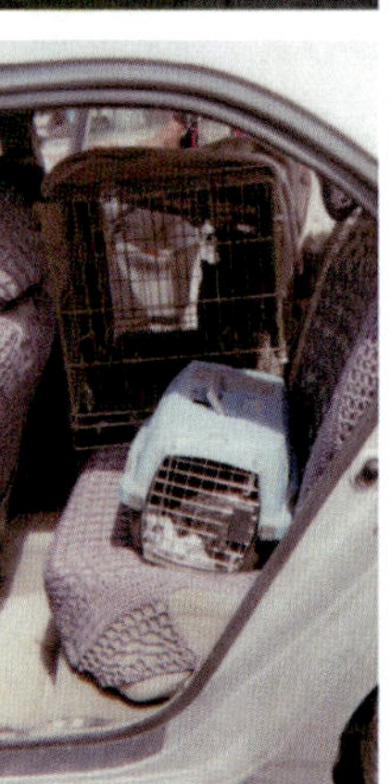
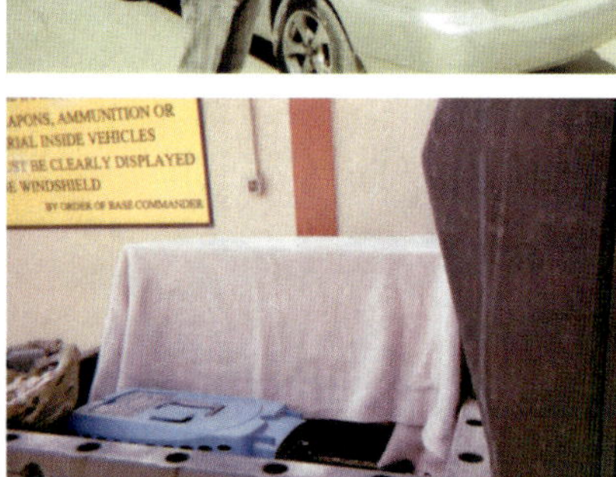
APONS, AMMUNITION OR
RIAL INSIDE VEHICLES
UST BE CLEARLY DISPLAYED
E WINDSHIELD
BY ORDER OF BASE COMMANDER

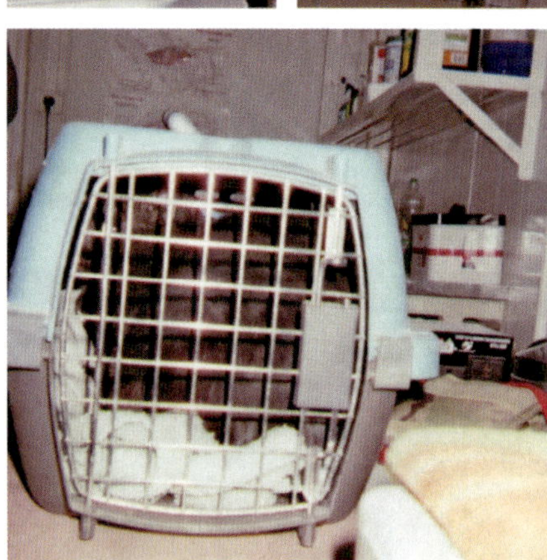

I

No Tail's existence during the three months after I placed him in that cab is not something that I would wish on any animal. In the span of a day, he had been caught in a trap, placed in a cab, and sent to a strange place with dozens of other cats and dogs in cages. He was a solitary cat that was now one of many in a throng of fur and claws.

His previous free existence that had allowed him to roam across acres of land had been shrunken down into a cage that allowed barely three-square feet of living space that he had to share with a litter box. It must have felt a lot like prison to him, without the comfort of at least understanding why he was there. The way he saw it, the person that he had finally decided to trust had betrayed him and then disappeared.

I wonder what part hurt worse. The sense of strangeness around him, or the lack of freedom, or the betrayal.

At the time No Tail was taken in, Now Zad housed about fifty cats and around a hundred dogs, as well as a couple of donkeys, a horse, and possibly a bird. The organization had been started in 2007 by a former Royal British Commando who had bonded with a dog during his deployment and had wanted to find a way to help fellow soldiers in similar situations. His mission turned into not just a way to reunite soldiers and their animals, but it also became the first and the largest animal rescue organization in Afghanistan.

No Tail's existence at the shelter would have been similar to a cat's life at most shelters in the US. Small cages, routine feedings and litter changes, with an overstretched staff doing the best they can. There would not have been an opportunity for play time, and it is not likely that there would have been much personal interaction at all. No Tail was not friendly under the best of circumstances, and these were far from the best of circumstances. I can imagine that some caregiver, after being swiped at through the bars yet again by the dark, angry cat that exuded rage might have wondered if some mistake had been made.

"This guy? He is being adopted? Really? Are you sure?"

This series of doldrums would have been punctuated with occasional physical health checks. Blood draws and vaccine boosters would not have added to a positive attitude for him. In order for a cat to qualify for transport to the states, they have to be given a clean bill of health. No parasites and no fatal communicable diseases.

This last requirement was one of our greatest concerns. We already knew that No Tail had FIV. Technically, FIV is a fatal disease, although it is usually fatal due to secondary effects and not the disease itself, but we were concerned that some overzealous quarantine monitor might classify this condition as a disqualifier.

In addition to the fear that his transfer would be denied, there was also the constant fear that he would escape and find himself in an unfamiliar location. Every time a cage door is opened and every time an animal is transported for a doctor visit, the possibility exists that the animal might rush the door or bite someone and escape. Eventually, we hoped that there would be a plane trip in his future as well, and the thought that he might escape during some transfer in Germany or the UAE was never far from our minds.

Perhaps the one consolation that I had was that No Tail would not be totally without friends at the clinic. Of course, I use the term friend here loosely. "Known quantity" might be a better term for it. Because in a cage nearby, was Monster.

An FCC volunteer had trapped Monster the week before we had finally trapped No Tail, and Monster was true to his name. He had been moved from the trap to the largest cage that the Feline Conservation Corps had in their little facility and had been scheduled for transport to Now Zad the previous week. He was so violent though that all of the volunteers had been too afraid to move him from the cage into a carrier for the trip. I knew who Monster was from my earlier association and had only discovered that he had been trapped when I came back to the facility to discuss how to get No Tail home.

The FCC supervisor had told me that they weren't sure what to do because they couldn't figure out how to get him from the cage into a carrier, and that he even made some of the volunteers nervous just to be in the clinic because if you even got close to the cage, he would launch himself at the bars and try to attack. They were on the verge of just opening the door and hoping he would leave on his own.

I looked at the massive beast in the cage and did some figuring. We were getting down to the wire and No Tail was still MIA. Robin had already given me the greenlight to bring a cat home, and by god I was going to rescue someone this time, if it killed me. Since No Tail was being elusive, I looked at Monster and pondered whether or not he would be interested in being No Tail's stand-in. Monster looked at me and wondered if I was interested in being his lunch.

After thinking about it carefully for my usual half a microsecond, I told the supervisor that I could take care of it. I said that the cage was big enough for a person to fit in it comfortably, so I would just crawl in the cage with Monster and sit down and write until he got used to a person's presence and calmed down.

The manager said, "Sure. That sounds like a great idea," and then slowly backed away from Monster and me, closing the door to the facility behind her.

My younger daughter had used this technique two years previously to befriend a shy foster cat that she was trying to socialize so that he could eventually be adopted. She had suggested the idea, so we had moved the cage to her bedroom, and she had spent hours over the next week, crawling into the cage and just sitting in there quietly. Even for our house, the sight of a cheerleader and a cat, sitting in a wire cage on the floor of a Paris-themed bedroom, doing chemistry homework together, was a bit surreal.

It had worked though. Of course, Jack had been a kitten at the time, not a banished demon from the fiery realm of Muspelheim. And I had left my cheerleader skirt at home.

What I did have was my pair of fast-rope gloves. Fast-roping is a method of rappelling out of a helicopter where you don't use harnesses or clips. You just drop a thick rope out of the chopper and then jump onto it and slide down it like a firehouse pole.

...If the firehouse pole is a hundred feet long, and is whipping around in the wind caused by the blades of the helicopter, and you have to jump from the door of a helicopter to grab onto it, and there is no safety gear.

But other than that, yeah, pretty much the same thing.

The gloves that you use for fast-roping are thicker than normal rappel gloves in order to handle the excessive friction that is generated. What I would have really liked to have had as I opened the door to Monster's cage was a pair of concertina gloves, or perhaps steel gauntlets and a suit of armor. I was certain that Monster had a bite force similar to that of an alligator and that my gloves would not offer as much protection as I hoped. I wondered what the letter home would look like if I died trying to calm down a feral cat.

Monster, for his part was being cooperative. He refrained from attacking the cage while I opened the door, but he was using every swear word that he knew as I slowly folded my body through the small opening. I did not speak Urdu, but I understood exactly what he had just said about my mother.

Once inside, I slowly closed and latched the door behind me. Monster almost immediately leapt out and swiped at me, but it wasn't an attack. It was simply a warning slap. I didn't react. I was cautious of how my face was exposed, but other than that, my intention was simply to ignore him. I pulled a book out of my cargo pocket and began reading.

For the next twenty minutes, Monster kept up a non-stop stream of hissed epithets and fanged threats, all while alternating between pressing himself against the cage as far away from me as he could, and advancing rapidly at me and slapping at my arms or legs.

It was clearly a fear reaction. That is what animals do when they are afraid. They hide, they threaten, they posture, they attack, they say things that are outside of their character or intent. I could have reacted to his actions, but I wouldn't have been reacting to Monster, I would have been reacting to his fear. It was necessary for both of our survivals at that moment, in the confined space we were in, that I maintain my ability to view him and his fear as two distinct things. If I had reacted to his fear instead of to him, it would have ended badly for both of us.

After twenty minutes, the hissing and the attacks lessened. After thirty minutes, they stopped altogether. After an hour of slowly moving an inch at a time, I was sitting next to him, and he was not fleeing to the other side of the cage. That was all it took. He did not become an affection seeker after that. He was still Monster. But at least he stopped trying to kill people.

So, the rest of the story is that morning when I walked out the front gate of the base and put No Tail in the cab, it was not one but two cages that I was carrying.

I don't know how reassuring that would have been to either one of them. I don't know if there would have been a sense of comfort in the familiarity of recognizing someone they knew, or if they hated each other and being in an unfamiliar situation with an enemy would have made it worse.

In my head, I picture them trash-talking me as they sat in cages next to each other.

"Yeah, so then he crawls in my cage, acting like he's gonna be my friend and everything, but then a few days later I wind up here and they're sticking needles in me!"

"You think that's bad? He brought me tuna. He knows I can't resist tuna. I knew he was up to something, and I was laying low, but then there it was. Tuna. That guy is such an ass."

"Hey, by the way, No Tail, what does "neuter" mean?"

11

Eventually No Tail got the all-clear. He had completed all the tests and all the shots, and his poop had been inspected and he had been observed and it was determined that he was fit to be a permanent resident of the United States. Now all that remained was to come up with the money.

It took us two months. Two months of him sitting there and waiting. Staring at the walls of his wire cage. Playing gin rummy with Monster.

Finally, in November of 2015, his trip was fully funded, and the only thing that remained was scheduling the flight. If you've never rescued a cat from a foreign country, even with the proper paperwork and funding, it is not as easy as logging on to the airline ticket site and ordering up a seat. An animal is cargo, which requires bills of lading. More paperwork. We were given a date for the flight and then it was changed. Another flight, another change. It started to feel like one of those movies where you feel like everything is finally going to come together the way it's supposed to and then they spring a surprise ending on you.

In December though, it was all finally arranged, and he began the last part of his journey. The reservations were made and then confirmed. Everything was checked and triple-checked. He was placed in an overseas carrier by the staff at Now Zad and taken by courier to the airport where he was logged in and loaded onto a plane. From Kabul, he was scheduled to fly to Kuwait, and then on to the US either through England or through Germany. The entire trip was supposed to take just under twenty four hours. We would get updates at each point in his flight, and then would get an estimated time of arrival once he left Europe so that we could be on hand to pick him up when he landed in Kansas City.

Hours passed and there were no updates. It should have been no more than five hours to Kuwait but after six hours there was nothing. At twelve hours we started calling and emailing.

We're not sure what is going on, they said. Everything is fine. We just need to figure out where he is.

Figure out where he is?!

What did that even mean? He's on the plane, right? And you didn't lose the plane, did you?

They weren't sure, but they said that they would let us know.

After a sleepless night, we got an update after more than twenty four hours telling us that they had found him on a plane in the United Arab Emirates. I pointed out that he wasn't even supposed to be going through the UAE. He is a cat in a box. It's not like he had too many drinks at the airport bar and got confused about which terminal he was supposed to board at his connecting airport.

To this day, we still do not know how it was that he wound up in the UAE. We never got confirmation that the original plane had gotten rerouted or that he had somehow been accidentally off-loaded in Kuwait and loaded mistakenly onto a different plane. What we do know is that he had to sit there in the cargo section of the airport for an entire day while they tried to figure out how to get things going again.

As far as No Tail was concerned, his life was just getting progressively worse. He had been put in a cage and kept there for almost three months. Then once he had probably begun to get used to his new routine, undesirable as it was, he had been taken yet again and loaded into a different box. He had been jostled about with unfamiliar sounds and smells. It had been a day since he had been given any food or water, and there was no litter box in his travel carrier so he had had to manage as best he could within the small, confined space.

And then, nothing.

We were told that once he was located at the airport in the UAE, he was given food and water, but there was nothing that could be done about the mess in the cage itself. Finally, two days after he left Kabul, he was back on another plane and enroute once again. Robin and I were given an arrival time for the terminal at the Kansas City International Airport. The following day, I left my office early and Robin met me at the airport, and we waited. We waited for two hours.

Because of the earlier mix-up we began to get understandably worried. Was it possible that they had lost him a second time? Were we about to get an email letting us know that he had somehow wound up in Toronto?

Then, from the back of cargo warehouse, we heard a sound. A sound that I recognized from many early mornings. A sound that would prompt my Aussie roommate to throw things at me and say, "Would you please get up and feed your cat?" A sound that Robin had never heard before but that she would grow to recognize. The look on her face was one of amazement.

"Is that a cat?!"

No. It wasn't "a" cat.

It was THE cat.

The loudest and angriest cat I had ever met. His howls of outrage caused everyone in the terminal to turn and stare. And somehow, I knew that he knew that I was there. He wasn't just shouting out in pointless rage, although he had plenty of that to go around. He was calling out to me. I don't know if he heard me or smelled me, and I don't know if he was promising revenge for what I had done or informing me that there had better be one helluva big plate of tuna waiting for him after this, but he was calling for me.

And as his carrier was finally wheeled out into the waiting area, another appellation was added to his string of mosts. The loudest cat and the angriest cat was also the smelliest cat. Three days in a small box without a litter pan will do that to you.

My eyes were watering as I finally got to speak to him for the first time, and whether they were tears of joy or simply tears from the fumes that were burning my eyes was hard to tell.

III

Robin has never met an animal that she didn't love, and there was no doubt that she was going to love No Tail, but that was assuming that she would ever be able to get close enough to even see him. When I say he smelled bad, I mean, imagine the worst smell that you could ever imagine and then magnify that by infinity. Imagine that you were an alien from the planet Smells Bad, located in the center of the Smelly Galaxy, and a factory on planet Smells Bad that manufactured industrial grade Foul Stench had just had a toxic chemical spill that was so bad it destroyed the entire Smelly Galaxy. If you can imagine that, you can begin to imagine how horrible and wretched he was.

The plan had initially been for me to follow Robin home in my car, and for No Tail and his carrier to ride in Robin's Expedition, but it was clear to see that unless we were attempting to euthanize Robin on the trip home, there was no way that he could be transported the way he was in a closed environment.

Fortunately, my car was a convertible. It wasn't big enough for his carrier, but with the top down we made it work and was decidedly the least lethal of the two options.

When we got home, we brought him upstairs to the triage bathroom in our previous home. When you work in animal rescue, there is always the "triage" bathroom. A place that can be easily cleaned and isolated from other pets or guests. Robin and I went into the bathroom, closed the door behind us, and opened the door to No Tail's carrier. For the first time in three days, he was able to step out of his box.

I would like to say that he immediately leapt into my arms and that I held him close, despite the fact that he was covered in three days' worth of filth and excrement, but the reality of the situation did not lend itself to that type of immediate connection. He was unquestionably happy to see us, that was not in doubt, but he was also very mad, and very aromatic.

We put him into the tub, which made him even less thrilled than he already was and began the arduous process of de-mucking him. Robin did most of the poop-removal while I mostly just petted his head and kept him occupied so that he wouldn't bite her. He was pretty good about it though. I think that he was probably miserable enough that he didn't have the energy to object.

When his initial bath was complete, we finally had a chance to look at him. He was still a beautiful cat, even with all of his wounds, but he was definitely thinner than he had been when we had parted in September.

"You've lost a little weight," I said to him.

Robin looked at me uncomfortably and turned away. "You should probably spend some time with him to get reacquainted," she said, and then left the room.

No Tail looked me up and down, surveying my own appearance which could be accurately described at that point as gaunt. I had passed thin about twenty pounds ago and was maybe another ten pounds away from being described as sickly.

You've lost a lot of weight yourself, his look said. At least I have an excuse. What cage have you been trapped in?

IV

The cage that I was trapped in at that moment had fallen just short of being a literal cage. As I explained earlier, the deployment I had just returned from was supposed to be part of a deal where the party of the first part, me, agreed to go to Afghanistan, and the party of the second part, the Army, agreed that when I got home I could remain in Kansas.

Our older daughter had already graduated high school and was now in college. Our younger daughter was a junior and we just wanted another year and a half so that she could graduate with her friends. I didn't think it was too much to ask. We weren't asking for forever. Just eighteen months. Then they were free to upend our lives and send us wherever they wanted.

The military loves supporting the military child. They will give your kids unit coins to show their appreciation for what the kids go through. They will let your kids stand next to you when you get promoted. Hell, they care so much about the kids that they officially designated an entire month as "The Month of the Military Child."

So, considering all the coins and certificates and a whole month of celebration my girls had received, I guess we were being greedy to ask for eighteen months.

For all of the missed birthdays. All of the missed recitals. For all of the phone calls interrupted by gun fire. For all of the memorials they attended. For the nightmares.

A coin is enough, right?

Apparently, the military thought so, because they had decided to change my assignment. Upon my return from Afghanistan, I was given thirty days to pack up my family and move across the country.

I started making phone calls that were initially polite but became more incensed over time. I went from reasoned appeals to accusatory statements that touched on topics like honesty and integrity. The response that I received was the time-tested reply that military officials have used for years. Their get out of jail free card. Every agreement or contract or assignment that the military makes always carries the possibility of nullification due to "needs of the Army."

It is elegant in its simplicity, and it is impossible to refute, since only the Army can decide what it needs.

I fought the reassignment orders and won a short reprieve that allowed me to push the timeline out another thirty days. I used that time to run, and every day, I watched the numbers on my scale tick backward.

When it finally became clear that the assignments branch was not going to change their position, I told them that I appreciated their position, but after careful consideration, I was afraid that I would have to decline their offer of reassignment. They were a bit put off and reminded me that it was not really an option. I told them that life is full of options.

True to their word, they completed the reassignment paperwork. True to my word, I chose the option not to go. On the day that I was supposed to report to my new unit, I received a confused phone call from the gaining S1, asking me where I was. I was confused as to why they would be confused. I told them that I was in Kansas. I informed them that they had my address, so they were welcome to stop by any time. If I wasn't home, I would be out running.

Tick, tick, tick, went the scale.

It's amusing now. Not exactly funny, but it has at least faded to the level of amusing. A lot of stupid things are amusing in hindsight.

V

The only smart thing that I did upon my return from Afghanistan was to return to my therapist. The one that had told me that going on another deployment was a monumentally bad decision, regardless of the motivation. She immediately noticed my weight loss, which did not exactly require Sherlockean observation skills. She asked me if I was trying to kill myself. My immediate answer was, "No."

Now if she had asked a slightly different question, something along the lines of "Are you trying to fade away?"

That might have elicited a different response.

There were a lot of psychoses tied up in my recent weight loss. I had always had issues with food, going all the way back to when my family had eaten purloined C rations out of cans heated over a propane cook stove. If you have ever gone hungry, or at least lived with the fear of going hungry, you view food differently than those who never went without.

It had nothing to do with appearance. Or at least not much. I look good at one eighty. I probably feel like I look my best at around one seventy. At one sixty I look…trim. By one fifty, the adjectives began to be less flattering.

I have a psychology background, so I am aware that food disorders are often precipitated by control problems. That definitely seemed to make the most sense in my case. I was rapidly learning how little control I had over anything. But in this one thing, I could reclaim some authority over at least one aspect of my life.

There was also the element of suffering, which had been a great comfort to me as a child. There is a line in the Goo Goo Dolls song, "Iris" that says, "When everything feels like the movies, yeah, you bleed just to know you're alive." So much of my life over the last few years felt unreal. Like something that you were watching on a screen, because this is not the kind of thing that happens to real people. So, in addition to the control element, this was also my way to bleed, except I was bleeding pounds instead of blood.

I was constantly hungry, and the hunger felt good because it hurt. The hungrier I became, the more it hurt. And at least when you hurt, you feel something. Feeling nothing means you're dead, and I felt like I was already drawing too close to that doorway. I should have been dead so many times over already. Musa Qalah or Kabul or Salman Pak or Baqubah or any of the times that IEDs didn't go off or grenades malfunctioned or guns jammed.

As many poor choices do, my weight loss did not begin as a conscious decision. I did not declare my intent to lose a third of my body weight. So, it is difficult to suss out what the real motive was behind it all. Maybe it was a race. I was familiar with those. Maybe my subconscious had declared, "Okay, here's what we're going to do. We're going to start losing weight. Survival, you've got pain on your side. The more it hurts, the more it's going to remind you that you're not dead. Death, you get all the rest. The more we lose, the easier it will be to fade away. Ready? Go!"

Tick, tick, tick, as I watched the numbers on the scale get lower and lower.

So that was the situation that I was in when Robin left the room after I made the comment about No Tail losing weight. Christmas was only two weeks away. By that time, I might be sent away from my family on my new assignment, half the country away, or I might be in the hospital, or I might even be in jail.

No Tail ate the food in his bowl as I told him all of this. Then after he was done, he laid down next to me. He listened carefully to what I had to say, and when I cried this time, he didn't bite me. He did, however, ask for more food. Over the next few days, he would rapidly regain the weight that he had lost during his travels. It would not be the last time that he set the example for me to follow.

VI

Shortly after No Tail's return, I became the only non-resident in a residential treatment facility in Kansas City. My therapist had been trying to get me admitted to a suicide prevention program for several weeks. I continued to insist that I was not suicidal.

Because all I was doing was running, right? I wasn't harming myself, I was just running. If anything, I was running away from death, not towards it. All of the images in my head. All of the voices. All of the shadows. I was running away from those things.

If I did wind up dying, the great thing about the route I had chosen was that it had a degree of plausible deniability to it. If I had simply suffered heart failure one day while out running, well there was nothing intentional about that. Or if the weight loss brough about some sort of organ failure because my body was starting to eat itself from the inside, no one could claim that it was on purpose.

"He was just a runner. He was into fitness. He certainly had no intention of dying. I mean, come on. He looked great. How could anyone have known?"

"...at least up until near the end, that is. Now that I think about it, yeah, he did look a little...worn, towards the end."

The problem with running away from your problems though is that your problems are all ultra-marathon runners as well. And they are better at it than you. Especially if death is one of your problems. Death is tireless and relentless and doesn't need to breathe. So, if you are running away from death, eventually it will catch up to you. And I was getting tired of running.

My therapist initially had threatened to admit me involuntarily to a treatment program, but I had responded to her in the same way that I had responded to my assignment orders. No Tail was home now though, and I had decided to stop fading away, so I agreed to admit myself to the program as long as I could complete it as a non-resident. She balked at this initially, but I explained three things to her.

First, one of the reasons she wanted me admitted as a resident was to keep me from harming myself. I assured her that I was not going to harm myself, but that if I was, there was no amount of safety measures that they could put in place in their facility that could stop me from doing it if that was my intent. Second, I had just come home from being separated from my family and the conditions that I lived in during that time were highly controlled, institutional conditions. Being placed back into a facility, regardless of the intent, would separate me from my family again and would place me back in an environment that stank of trauma. And finally, I had a cat at home. I wasn't going to abandon him again.

She did not like any of the three points, but she did agree that something was better than nothing, so I drove myself to the facility the next day and checked in. I was nervous as I stepped through the security doors, and immediately began developing a plan in case this had all been a ruse and now that I was in the facility they were going to attempt to confine me as a full time resident.

They did not, and I was saved from the need to creatively fashion tools out of therapy dough and plastic forks and engineer a MacGyver style escape from the facility.

I did not find the therapy at the facility to be particularly useful. I disliked the time that was spent sitting around and listening to positive aphorisms that were supposed to help us reframe our trauma. The art therapy and entertainment group seemed pointless, like perhaps I had signed up for a first-grade craft group instead of a suicide therapy program. The part that really ticked me off though was the reasoning therapy.

I know. When you have rage issues, becoming enraged by the tools that you are being given to work through the rage is not the best reaction. But as I spoke with the therapist about this, I felt like I was back in the emergency room in California, trying to explain to the doctor that my ankle was broken. I felt like they had a diagnosis and a treatment model already prepared, and they were trying to make my situation fit their treatment, instead of tailoring the treatment to fit the situation.

Conceptually, I don't disagree with Cognitive Reasoning Therapy, or its many derivatives. When utilized properly, within its scope of operations, it can be a very useful tool. The very abridged underlying theory is that we often struggle to properly link cause and effect, which can then create unhealthy coping mechanisms.

A simple illustration is that, for example, a soldier is killed in an IED explosion. The officer in charge of identifying terrorists cells and stopping IED attacks blames himself and says, "If only I had worked harder or had been better at my job or had not hesitated, my friend would still be alive. It is my fault that my friend is dead."

CRT forces a person to reframe the trauma statement in a more accurate manner. "A terrorist killed my friend. I am sad that he is dead. I dislike situations where I don't have control. The idea that someone could kill another of my friends, and I would not have control over it is scary. Therefore, I would rather blame myself for what happened than live with the fear that there are things like this out there that I cannot control. But the truth is that there are things that I cannot control. And the truth is that I did not kill my friend."

It is far too complex to encompass it in three paragraphs. If you are struggling with trauma, do not try and use this summary to therapize yourself. Go find a therapist.

The point is that it is easier to reframe or restate singular incidents. The more singular and less complex the incident, the better. The question that I asked my therapist was, "Which of my traumas would you like me to reframe?" Naively, they said, "Well, whichever one is creating the source of your depression and anxiety. Or if there is more than one, write down two or three of them."

I asked them, "What if there are hundreds?"

They didn't have an answer for that.

So, I continued to attend my daily, all-day treatment sessions, but without much investment in the outcome. There were however, two positives that did come out of the program. The first was that when my assignments branch found out that I was in a suicide prevention program for soldiers with PTSD, they put my orders on hold. It wasn't an end to the orders war, but it was at least a cease-fire.

The other positive was that I had finally accepted that this was not a problem that I could solve on my own. Fortunately, a twelve-pound, furry therapist had just moved in with us full-time.

No Tail Settles In

His reaction to the cab driver's unusual appearance was muted in comparison to his reaction to the meaty thing that had accosted him on the train into Manhattan. If the rest of the morning continued like this, seeing the Loch Ness monster in the fountain in Central Park on his lunch break might draw no more than a disinterested shrug of the shoulders from him. Andrew supposed that when the bizarre becomes the norm, it begins to lose its ability to shock you.

FROM, **"SOMETHING ODD HAPPENS,"** BY THAD KRASNESKY

Birds of
Missouri

I

He was still a very stinky therapist though.

We mentioned the smell already, right? And in case we didn't emphasize it enough, it bears repeating. No Tail had two baths that first day, but the smell was so ingrained in him that I began to wonder if it was something that we would ever completely get rid of. It had already begun to seep out of the bathroom and into the adjoining bedroom, and after spending time with him in his bathroom, you would come out feeling like you carried the odor on you and needed to shower, like a non-smoker spending twenty four hours in the slot machine pit of a casino and never being able to get the smell of cigarettes out of their sweater again.

After about a week though, it did gradually dissipate, and he was able to be moved from the bathroom into the more spacious bedroom. This gave him more space to roam around in, and it also allowed us to sit on the bed with him, and even sleep over night with him so that he had someone to snuggle with.

He was absolutely the same cat that I had first met half a world away though. Regardless of his climate-controlled surroundings and heated bed and three catered meals a day, not to mention his constantly curated litter box, he was still a semi-feral cat with an over-sized voice, and over-sized anger.

He was hesitant at first to accept affection from new people, but it was not long before he was as comfortable being petted by Robin or my daughters as he was being petted by me. Once he was accustomed to their presence, he began to demand attention the same way that he used to demand food. He did not need it constantly, but when he heard people in the house and decided that their time would be better spent tending to him, he would announce it loudly, and he would not be silenced until you gave in to his demands and came in to pet him.

Only on the head though. He was often satisfied just to have someone sitting in the room with him without any touching at all, but if you did touch him it had to be only on his head. If your hand strayed toward his neck, beyond his field of vision, you would get bitten. If you came into his room after he had summoned you with his howling, and tried to stroke his flanks, you would get bitten.

He would accept touch from people he could see, but all contact was still viewed as a potential attack. Contact that came outside his field of vision would be met accordingly, and even when he laid down to rest, he would always do so with his eyes on the other person in the room. It didn't matter that you might have sat down with him for the last hour, petting his head or just sitting quietly and reading a book. When he relaxed and curled up beside you, he would always be facing you, and even when he slept in his room by himself, he would do so facing the door.

It is a common symptom of PTSD brought on by combat. The need to ensure that you have eyes on anyone else in the room and that you never turn your back on a person or a possible entrance that might present an avenue of attack. It such a common symptom in fact that it winds up being overly dramatized and overused by a lot of people in the entertainment industry to the point that it becomes annoying. Some people that I have known have internalized the concept as some sort of integral aspect of manliness to the point that they make a production of loudly proclaiming how they always check exits when they enter a building and never sit with their backs to the door, but when you speak to them you find out that they never even served in a combat environment but wear this symptom of trauma experience like they wear old military gear they purchase from a pawn shop.

As a contrarian point of pride, I would often do the exact opposite. I would actively choose a seat in a restaurant that intentionally placed my back to the door, because I never wanted to be associated with the "I saw it once in a movie" veterans. Most of the time it didn't really bother me but sometimes it made me nervous as hell, but I did not want my fear or my trauma to define me. What I would not realize until much later was that, whether you sit facing a door because your trauma makes you do it, or whether you sit with your back to the door to deny your trauma, either way you are allowing your trauma to control your actions. Either decision could be the right decision, but it was being made for the wrong reason, and the right decision for the wrong reason is still a dick move. I was being just as performative as the people I was trying to avoid being identified with.

I doubted that No Tail had seen many Hollywood movies though, and even if he had, I doubted if he would have cared what someone thought about his decisions on where to sit. He wasn't trying to look tough, or nonchalantly anti-tough. He was just trying to survive.

For two weeks we kept No Tail isolated in his room. That is the standard time frame in cat rescue integration. Whenever we coach people on how to integrate a new cat or dog into their home, we always tell them, two weeks. It gives the other animals in the household time to become aware of the newcomer, and it gives the newcomer time to realize there are other animals in the space they now reside in. This acclimation period lets them smell each other through the door, and they might even begin to interact with each other vocally or even physically if there is any space underneath the door that separates them. In best case scenarios you might even see them begin to play, which usually makes life so much easier when the door is finally opened.

After two weeks, then you begin a controlled and supervised period of integration. You let the pets interact and if there are any signs of aggression you redirect them. If it persists, you separate them and try again the next day.

At the time that we brought No Tail home, we had five resident cats, and a dog. We had our oldest cat, Breve, a twelve year old orange and white male that Robin had found in the road with a broken leg and had rescued during my deployment to Iraq in 2003. Luna, a low-slung dirigible diva black female cat that was about four years old and was a behavioral rescue. Salem, a large, black, four-year-old house panther who was Luna's therapy buddy. Jack, the aforementioned shy boy that my daughter had socialized, and who had wound up deciding to stay with us instead of being adopted out. And then there was the newest addition, Phryne, an eight month old high-strung female black cat that had turned out to be a foster that was unadoptable, so Robin had added her to our clowder while I was away.

We had also just lost our senior female calico, Olivia, in September of 2015, a month before I came home and three months before No Tail had arrived. She had been about eighteen years old, and had been rescued at four weeks old when she had been found abandoned, with a severe external hernia that had needed surgery, so Robin had taken her in.

Additionally, Robin had fostered a litter of kittens recently while I was gone, so although there were only five cats in residence at the time, the house had recently held as many as twelve, and the smells of all of the fosters and people that had passed through our doors, to the nose of a sensitive feline, would have been a lot of information to take in. For one coming from an austere, outside environment, it would have been more than just new. It would have bordered on alien.

There did not seem to be any outward signs of distress though. He was active and gained his travel weight back. He had zero issues adjusting to the litter box so there was no inappropriate peeing. Our primary concern though was how he would react to the five cats once they were all introduced. We expected that there would be conflict. We figured there would be territorial issues about favorite spots on the couch or which side of the food mat was whose. We were prepared even for the likelihood that there would be some aggression and scuffles before the new hierarchy had been established and everyone settled into their adjusted roles.

In the two week acclimation period, we had had the normal amount of "new animal" energy pass back and forth between No Tail's bedroom suite and the cats outside. There had been occasional growling, but mostly it had been a matter of indifference on No Tail's part, and casual curiosity from the resident cats. We anticipated the normal amount of posturing when we finally opened the door.

What we had not anticipated was murder.

11

There really is no other way to describe it. We have seen animals fight before. We have seen the assertion of dominance and even the need to physically injure another creature. Only in the wild had we seen animals act with the sole intent of killing the other animal in front of them.

We had never seen this kind of behavior in our own home, but we saw it that night, in early January of 2016. When we first released No Tail into the general population, he did not hesitate. The indifference that he had demonstrated disappeared, or perhaps had only been a façade in the first place. He went on an immediate hunt and kill mission. The other cats in the house were unprepared for the fury that had just been unleashed upon them.

No Tail went after the first target he saw, which happened to be our dog. He was not attempting to dominate anyone or claim any territory. He was there to kill, and that was it.

Robin and I are both well-prepared and well-rehearsed in breaking up potentially dangerous fights. We know all the tricks of the trade and have all of the necessary tools. We were not prepared for this. We had the equivalent of carrying mace to ward off a mugger. What we needed was a swat team trained in taking down a terrorist cell.

Robin grabbed for Lola, but I do not know if her intervention would have been enough to stop the attack, had Jack not peeked around the corner to see what was going on. When No Tail saw the other cat, he left off attacking Lola and shot toward Jack. Jack knew immediately that he was in trouble and tried to flee, but No Tail was as fast as he was focused. He leapt onto Jack and went for the kill.

With no time to implement normal procedures, Robin grabbed a large comforter that was lying across the back of the couch and threw it over the two cats. The weight of the comforter contained the attack and slowed it down, but it did not stop it entirely. We attempted to insert ourselves between the two cats by pressing down on the blanket and pushing, but No Tail slashed and bit through the thick winter comforter, drawing blood from both Robin and me. We then had to resort to using another blanket for additional padding and a cardboard box to slowly pry them apart beneath the first blanket. Once they were separated, we were able to lift one side of the blanket up and release Jack.

Robin and Isabelle focused on checking Jack out for injuries and reassuring him while I managed to wrap No Tail up in the blanket like a murderous Santa sack and bring him back upstairs to his room. When I dumped him out on the bed, he had that same look in his eyes that he had when he had attacked Monster eight months previously. Again, I had a concern that he might become confused and attack me as a target of opportunity.

This was the first time that I saw a foreshadowing of what No Tail would eventually become. Not in the murderous rage in his eyes, but in the fear beneath the rage. It wasn't the other animals that he was afraid of. It was the rage itself. Rage is a terrifying thing to see, but it is also a frightening thing to experience. It is like remaining conscious while your body is possessed, but there is no holy water you can throw on yourself to exorcise it. Demons like rage and depression and fear are not easily banished with a few words and a sprinkling of salt, because they are not an external intruder, and the hell that they come from is inside you. It is the self, possessing the self.

When I had seen this rage in No Tail when we were in Afghanistan, I did not get the opportunity to see the fear that followed. He had run off, which is what he tried to do now, but now there was nowhere for him to hide. The rage infused every ounce of his body, but the fear in his eyes told me that he felt more trapped by this emotion that he was unable to control than he had ever felt while being held in a physical cage. Eventually he tucked himself into the back of the closet, and I went to check on Lola and Jack.

Fortunately, and somewhat miraculously, no one was seriously injured. There were a few deep scratches but nothing that would require an emergency room visit.

The dynamics around the door to No Tail's room changed after that. The cats and the dog avoided the door as much as possible, and when they did have to pass by it, they would cross to the opposite side of the hall. There were no more exploratory sniffs or offers of friendship. There was a monster in the room, and they weren't sure why dad had brought it home, but they were going to steer well clear of it.

No Tail had a new behavior pattern as well. Where before he had been content to wait for people to come to him and would mostly ignore the steps of the other animals passing his door, he now began to try breaking out.

III

A lot of cats will claw at a door to let you know that they want out. No Tail however was a strong and independent cat and had no intention of waiting for you to let him out. He decided that he was going to dig his way out like he was in a fifties prison movie. The carpet would be the first casualty.

At first, we tried to discourage this by using different cat products on the carpet in front of the door but none of them worked. It was not long before we had to accept the fact that we were going to have to replace the carpet in that bedroom, since he was shredding it so much. In a matter of days though, we realized that he wasn't simply scratching the carpet and tearing it. He was systematically removing it. He completely detached a section of carpet that extended about four feet to either side of the door and another three or four feet back into the room.

With the carpet gone, we assumed that he would give up, but he continued right on through the padding that was underneath the carpet. We thought surely he would have to stop then but he went even further and began to dig into the wood of the subfloor itself.

At that point we had to institute drastic measures. The carpet was ruined but we had a very real concern that he would not stop until he had gone through the floor and then through the ceiling below. Although that seemed a bit cartoonish, the more realistic concern was that he would start to create splinters that would catch in his paws or his mouth.

The solution was as innovative as it was unattractive. We got a sheet of quarter inch steel and bolted it to the floor in front of the door.

If you have ever walked into someone's house and seen questionable flooring choices, or design elements that you felt were tasteless, or maybe even had a neighbor that left car parts or appliances in their yard that you were concerned might bring down the value of houses on your street, be assured that few things say "tacky" as succinctly as walking into someone's house and seeing a piece of steel bolted into a bare spot on the floor. Now of course, this wasn't in any of the spaces that guests would normally see, but still, it was a sight to behold.

Even this did not stop him right away. As we have mentioned, No Tail was persistent. He was not convinced that he would not be able to claw through the metal, and so he initially maintained his attempt to dig his way out, unabated by the new obstacle. And if you think fingernails on a chalkboard is a sound to put your teeth on edge, imagine what it sounds like when someone takes eight tiny daggers and begins to scrape them across a sheet of steel, over and over again.

For days, the other cats looked like characters in a horror movie where the creature has been locked behind what should be an impenetrable door, but everyone exchanges nervous glances as they wonder if it is going to hold. Even Robin and I wondered. It did not seem possible that he would be able to actually tunnel his way through steel, but we were beginning to believe that there was not anything that lay outside his capability, and we actively discussed what we would do if that measure failed.

After a few days, he finally gave up. I don't know if he realized that he wasn't making headway, or if it just did not feel good on his claws. Whatever the reason, the door had finally been secured.

This did nothing though to address the bigger problem of how to integrate a murderer into an urban cat clowder. No Tail suggested that the best solution would be to just get rid of the other cats, or to let him out so that he could take care of it if we were too squeamish. He was the only one that was excited about that option. For the time being, what we wound up doing was creating a rotational schedule to ensure that he got at least two hours of people time every night.

It was not ideal. It was certainly an improvement over his previous life in Afghanistan. He had all the food he could eat and clean water to drink and soft beds to sleep on and a temperature controlled environment that never got too hot or too cold. He received the best medical care that money could buy.

And two hours was less people time than what the other cats got, but it was certainly more than he had been used to in Afghanistan. He wanted more though, and so did we. We wanted him to be a part of our lives, not just a chore that needed tending to. We wanted to sit with him while we watched movies or played games or ate dinner. We wanted him to be able to sleep with his people if that is what he desired. And we also wanted him to have space. He was an indoor cat now for sure. Not only was it healthier for him, but the local environment would not be familiar to him, and with all of the change he had gone through, it was unlikely that we would ever see him again if he got out.

He should at least have run of the house though. There was plenty of space inside for him to explore, and everyone would be happier if we could find a way to make it happen. And we did, but it would take eighteen months, and the intervention of a small, orange kitten that had a survival story of his own.

IV

As we tried different approaches and methods to help No Tail control and moderate his own anger issues, I was continuing to work on mine as well. We were both equally successful in making almost no headway in controlling the demon inside. And while we could keep No Tail separated from the other cats and at least moderate the effects of his anger, there was no way to lock me away from the rest of society.

I began to seek out confrontations more and more. I had rules though. I couldn't just pick any fight. I had to pick a righteous fight because in my head I was still the good guy. Thankfully, though, there was never a shortage of rude and aggressive bullies out there to create a release valve for me. In most cases, these situations resolved quickly because bullies are cowards. Evil almost always is. They bluster and expect no one will call them out, and when someone does, they tuck their tail and run. In numbers though, when they think that they have the advantage, they can still be dangerous.

The actual altercations were few and far between and were never satisfying. The anger inside never felt completely sated.

Then on the way to my office one day, I saw a group of three young men on motorcycles. They were popping wheelies on the highway and harassing an older woman in a car. They would swarm her vehicle and drive directly at her, causing her to swerve and almost run off the road.

My righteous indignation immediately hit critical mass. Surely no one could call this unjustified. They outnumbered the woman. They were younger than her. They were a physical and possibly even mortal threat to many people. And they were actively involved in an activity that was a clear violation of the law. My intervention would not only be justified, it would be lauded. The rage demon inside me sat up and started drooling.

My first reaction was to intervene, but reason was still conscious enough to point out that it was necessary to contact the police to report the incident first. The dispatcher did not seem to be too concerned but they did at least get the information from me. As I was on the phone with the dispatcher, the three cyclists made a right turn onto a side road, and I followed.

I suspect that the riders might have thought at that point that I was following them because they then made another abrupt turn and entered the highway. After quickly exiting the highway and reversing direction, it became apparent to the riders that I was indeed following them, and they began to then address their actions toward me. One of the riders raced ahead and then turned and drove at my vehicle in the oncoming lane, attempting I assume to intimidate me into crashing my vehicle or to at least cease following them.

I was still on the phone with the police dispatcher during all of this, updating the roads we were on and the direction of travel, and describing the illegal actions that they were taking. The dispatcher recommended to me on several occasions that I should break off following them for my own safety and let the police handle it. I pointed out to her that it was highly unlikely that the police would be able to locate them without an update on their location.

My unreason began to masquerade as reason and explained to me that the best solution would be to convince the drivers to remain in one location long enough for the police to arrive and resolve the matter. Not looking for a fight. Just trying to be a responsible citizen, right?

I started gesturing to the riders to pull their vehicles over and requesting that they await the arrival of the local constables. There is a possibility that some of my gestures were of a less than friendly variety, and some of my requests might have been construed by some as physically aggressive and possibly insulting.

After some hesitation, they complied. They pulled into the parking lot of a church and stopped at the far end. I pulled into the center of the lot and stopped. I told the police what our location was and then turned off my phone and got out of the car.

I was practically glowing when I stood up, and it's possible I might have even been laughing. I was as high on adrenaline as I had been on any of the combat operations I had engaged in while I was deployed. Something was about to happen. There was going to be a confrontation. I had no idea what the outcome was going to be. Someone was undoubtedly going to be hurt, and there was a non-zero chance that it was going to be me, but right would have its day, and the defender of little old women in cars from hooligan motorcyclists would have his hill.

There was no plan. I had no idea how I was going to fight three young men on motorcycles. People who have served with me or have known me to any degree will tell you that I rarely have a plan. I see an action that needs to be done, and I act. The details will get sorted out along the way.

One of the riders rode directly at me, and I suspect that he assumed I would jump out of the way, which would have been a reasonable reaction from someone operating on the self-preservation principle, but since that part of my software had glitched out years ago, I didn't move. He braked and swerved at the last minute, and for a moment I thought he would handle the situation for me by simply crashing into the curb, but he regained control of his bike and returned to his two friends.

One of the other riders rode more slowly toward me and circled me and my vehicle. I waited for him to move towards me as the other one had, but he did not. He returned to the other two and the three of them sat there speaking for a moment and then revving their engines like someone who had watched Mad Max a few times too many and had decided that they wanted to join the mutant side of this dystopian encounter.

Since the police had still not arrived, and with no other options available to me, I started walking toward them.

That is completely untrue of course. There were countless other options available to me. Almost every one of them was a better option than the one I chose to pursue. But when you want to do a thing anyway, it is easy to decide that your way is the only way.

I got halfway across the parking lot before the riders turned their bikes and sped off.

I stood there, staring at them, and almost immediately started shaking. My body was so hyped up on the anticipation of conflict that when that outlet was removed, it was like plugging a two twenty power cord into a high voltage transformer.

I tried functioning at my office that day, but by lunchtime the shaking had not stopped, and I had to do something. Something was running of course. I went for a run. I don't know how far I ran. I just know I ran until I was shaking from exhaustion instead of from repressed anger.

That evening, when the angry shaking threatened to return, I laid down in my sleeping bag on the floor of No Tail's room. He climbed into the sleeping bag with me, and we both stayed up most of the night, drifting off occasionally and waiting for the sun to rise.

V

The sleeping bag had been Robin's suggestion. When I had come home from my deployment in 2004, I had begun talking in my sleep. Except it wasn't just talking. It was arguing. It was shouting. Occasionally it was sobbing.

Imagine lying in bed, completely relaxed, asleep, dreaming puffy, white cloud dreams, when suddenly the person next to you starts screaming. Once or twice would be jarring. It would be that uncomfortable thing that you laugh about a few years later. Somewhere around the tenth time it happens, it becomes disturbing. And by the time it starts happening multiple times a week for over a year and you are well into the triple digits, it simply becomes exhausting.

As troubling as that sounds, Robin has informed me that the shouting and the sobbing is not the worst part though. According to someone that has lived it for most of her adult life, the worst moments are when I begin talking in a conversational tone of voice with someone who isn't there, especially when those conversations are taking place in a language you don't understand.

When these night incidents began, Robin would attempt to wake me up. She would talk to me or shake me and sometimes I would wake up, but sometimes I would not. I would just go on talking, having my conversation with some dream person in my mind, in Arabic or some other language, responding to the person that wasn't there, but not responding at all to her.

She would occasionally pick up her phone and record these moments, partly out of curiosity to hear me translate what I had been saying, but also out of a need to prove to me and to others that it was really happening, and that someone in this relationship might be crazy, but it wasn't her. I can tell you that it is disconcerting and creepy to see yourself in a video, engaging in an extended conversation while you are asleep. I can only surmise that seeing it in person, happening to someone you love in real time, is even creepier than watching it on a recording.

The remarkable quickly becomes unremarkable when it becomes the norm. Eventually the trauma reactions became mundane. While we were living in Arizona, at one point I began a series of dreams where I would speak for hours on end in French to someone that was apparently a Spanish monk. After the first couple of nights, I slept on the couch. It was a reaction no different than the response someone might have to their partner snoring too loudly.

As a couple of paragraphs in a story, that might be interesting or possibly even amusing. But now try to imagine that experience not as a paragraph in a story, but as your life. Every single night of your life. World without end, amen.

Sleep deprivation is used as a type of torture. How would you react if your life was torture?

And those were only the nightmares that happened while I was asleep.

Relationships with broken people are appealing when it is presented on a movie screen and is accompanied by its own soundtrack. They are dramatically romantic when you are able to walk away after the lights go up and the credits roll. The reality of it is much less grand.

Almost anything can be endured for an hour and a half, but life is not so conveniently condensed. There are no commercial breaks. There are no montages that speed up years of healing into a digestible four minute inspirational moment.

Imagine for a moment that you have a stone in your shoe. It rubs on your foot every time you take a step. It would not be many steps before you stopped to take off your shoe and shake out the stone. Now imagine you were told that you were going to have to walk with that stone in your shoe for the rest of your life. We can talk about love and devotion until Byron comes home, but the poetry of it all fades quickly once blisters form and your shoe fills with blood.

Except sometimes the stone isn't in your shoe, it's in your heart.

It is tempting at times like that to take off your heart, shake out the stone, and move on.

And of course, Robin was not the only one living the life. My kids had to deal with it as well. My rage was never directed against my family. I never became violent with them. But that doesn't mean they were immune to it. Actions taken in anger impact everyone, even if they are not the recipients of it.

Similar to the incident with the motorcycles, I once encountered a reckless driver who was actively waving a gun at people. I followed him, placing the mask of "protecting people from an armed threat" over the smile of rage beneath. When I had cornered him, he got out of his vehicle and I got out of mine, with the intention of disarming him.

The police had somehow gotten involved and had arrived while we were getting out of our cars. My assumption was that they would arrest the guy with the gun that had been pointing at people. I became shocked and my rage grew as I realized that the police were actually on the verge of arresting me.

I was already redlining pretty hard, and although I wasn't trying to "fade away" anymore, being shot by a cop while doing what I thought was right might have been an appealing hill to die on. And No Tail wasn't there to talk me out of it.

My daughter, however, was.

She had been in the car with me the entire time and was now calling out to me to just get back in the car and leave. I had either not taken her safety into consideration, or I had egotistically determined that I was capable of protecting her so it was okay to put her at risk like that. I would like to say this was an isolated incident, but I think we have already established that it was not. All of the rescue work in the world doesn't make up for putting your family into situations where they might need to be rescued because of your actions.

I was the stone in the shoe, and it wasn't just Robin that was getting blisters.

And, Isabelle and Rachael, if I have not apologized to you for that before, I am so sorry.

I didn't have a solution or a cure for moments like this. All I had was my running. The moments of conscious rage were something that had to be swallowed down, and hopefully digested before I wound up vomiting it back out onto everyone around me.

We did have a response though for the nightmares. The response that we developed for those developed organically one time when I commented to Robin that what I really wanted to do was to just take out my sleeping bag and go sleep outside.

Robin asked me if I had the nightmares when I was deployed. It had never occurred to me until she asked the question, but the answer was that I did not. For some reason, my mind had decided that if I was home, my dreams would be filled with nightmares, but while I was deployed and actually living the nightmares, what little sleep I got would be relatively dream free.

So, Robin suggested that I try it at home. Perhaps we could trick my brain into thinking it was still deployed. And it worked.

From that point on, when things would get too bad, I would get my sleeping bag out and sleep on the floor.

And that is why No Tail and I wound up on the floor of his room in my sleeping bag, after my moment of unconsummated rage.

VI

Although No Tail's integration in those first few months was not ideal, it was gratifying to see new parts of his personality begin to emerge that were not tainted by fear or rage. Whereas in Afghanistan, it required caution and patience, even from people he knew well, to get close to him, after he decided who his people were, he leaned in hard. Literally.

He showed himself to be a head-bumper of prodigious vigor. If you leaned in to speak to him, he would lower his head and launch his forehead at you as if somewhere in his ancestorial past was a billy goat, or possibly even a rhinoceros.

He also became our constant shadow any time he was out of his solitary confinement suite. In Afghanistan, he had constantly hung around the periphery of people, demonstrating a desire to be part of our world, but always hanging back out of fear. In his new home in Kansas, the fear quickly left him. Anywhere you happened to be, he would be there, without hesitation.

He went full cat. If Robin was doing yoga for her personal practice or preparing for a class or workshop she was going to teach, he would be right there, in the middle of the mat. If I was writing, he would lean against my leg and drape his head over onto my notebook or laptop so as to cause all productive efforts to cease. If we were opening mail, he would place himself on top of the stack of envelopes and declare that anything that did not direct attention to him was obviously junk mail and could be ignored. Even taking showers, he would sit on the edge of the sink, staring through the glass door, which was endearing, in spite of the intensity of his gaze that gave the experience just a note of voyeurism to it.

Cooking was a massive challenge. Although we had a well-documented record of No Tail's fondness for tuna, we discovered that preference did not equate to pickiness. He would eat anything. His actions were not dissimilar from what children who have lived with food insecurity demonstrate when placed into a situation where food is abundant. He became an indiscriminate gorger of anything he could get his teeth on. If it was not nailed down, he would grab it and run, devouring most of what he stole before even bothering to decide whether or not he liked it.

Bread was one of his favorite comfort foods. After several stolen loaves of bread and bags of scones wound up leaving tell-tale, Hansel and Gretel trails of crumbs to his hiding spot beneath the parson's chairs, we learned that the pantry door could never be left open. If Robin and I were having a conversation or watching a movie and suddenly realized that No Tail was not glued to our side, we would look at each other and instantly realize that someone must have violated the pantry door protocol. This realization would be followed by a Keystone Cops chase scene where we would run to the kitchen and then attempt to chase No Tail down to retrieve whatever remained of his latest carbohydrate kill.

It was during one of these chase scenes that we discovered No Tail's incredible leaping ability. The counters in our home at that time were standard counter height, which is three feet. Our ceilings were ten-foot ceilings. The cabinets in the kitchen did not go all the way to the ceiling. They had been left with a one-foot gap at the top to provide a decorative space into which we had placed a design element consisting of strands of grape vine, wine plates, and strings of lights.

Having discovered that our tailless shadow was not seated next to us, Robin and I got up and raced to the kitchen. The culprit heard us coming and leapt onto the counter, and then, in amazement we watched as he leapt six feet from the countertop to the top of the cabinets, still holding onto his prize. The leap itself was within the range of a standard house cat. Six feet, while impressive, is not an earth-shattering accomplishment.

What made it so impressive to us was the absolute ease with which he executed the jump. In trying to explain it to other people we would use terms like "explode" or "teleport" to communicate the effortless nature of his physical prowess. One moment he was on the counter, the next he had simply willed himself into a twelve inch space, six feet above him.

After getting over our amazement, our effort to rescue the bread quickly morphed into a concern for the twisted obstacle course of vines and lighting and breakable ceramics that No Tail was now traversing. In our minds, we could see the entire thing plummeting downward in a tangled mess, breaking the plates, destroying the decoration, and likely injuring No Tail in the process. No Tail, however, was completely unconcerned about the potential for disaster, and openly scoffed at our consternation as he explored his newly discovered refuge for a suitable place to sit down and finish his snack. Without the slightest disturbance to our cabinet frippery, he found a spot to curl up in where he could maintain direct eye contact with us as he casually munched on his bread.

VII

The top of the cabinets became his sanctuary after that. It was his robber's hide-out where he would go when he stole forbidden food. It was also his refuge when it was bedtime and we were ready for him to go back to his room. There were more than a few occasions where I had to get out the ladder to retrieve him from his perch when his rotation time was complete.

We had initially pondered ways to discourage him from going up there, but we quickly gave in and even wound up putting a cat bed up there for him, nestled among the sparkling lights and the coils of woody vines.

Even though No Tail had become relaxed and secure enough to spend time with family without hesitation, it took him a little longer to warm up to other people. He would always seek high ground when strangers came over. That at first had been the top of the stairs, but now it was the top of the cabinet. Guests would come over in the evenings for dinner or to play board games and would often have a moment of surprise when they spotted a pair of eyes staring down at them from nine feet up in the air.

Even that hesitation soon disappeared. He became a regular attendee at our game nights. Ideally, he would want to sit in someone's lap while we played, but since most games require some form of movement and he did not like to be disturbed, he would usually find a place on the table to perch and observe.

We also discovered that No Tail expected to be included in the games as well, particularly if the game had playing pieces. He would watch people move their pawns or figures around the board and would decide that he needed his own playing piece, at which point he would just pick one up in his mouth and walk off. We learned though, that if we gave him his own pawns at the beginning of the game, he was less likely to disturb the board. Many game nights would be spent with No Tail sitting on the table next to us and our friends, perched on top of his own plastic playing pieces. And no matter what the final tally was on any of the games we played, it was clear to everyone who No Tail thought the real winner was.

No Tail Lets Go of his Rage

"You and I don't come from the same world!" he shouted. "You have no idea what I've been through!"

"You're right," El replied. "I'm sorry for what you had to endure. I won't pretend to understand it. But today, right now, this is the world that we have to live in. You can't live in two worlds, so pick one! If you want to live, you'll choose this one, because if you choose to live in the past, how is that any different from dying?"

From, **"Designers"**, by Thad Krasnesky

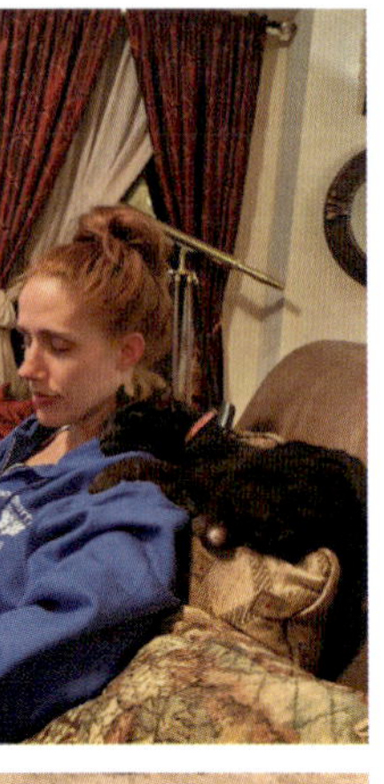

I

For eighteen months the rotation schedule in the house meant that at around five o'clock, the other five cats would get put away in the master bedroom and one of the other guest rooms, and we would release No Tail from his two-room suite. No Tail began to develop a less artificial lifestyle that allowed him to become included in more family oriented events. We also hoped that as he began to become more comfortable with his surroundings and get to know the other cats through their scents around the house, he would become more friendly and less murdery.

It was an improvement, but still not ideal. I hated the way that he would call out to us during the day when he wanted to be out with the family and do family things. It hurt me that we could not figure out a way to fully integrate him. For a year and a half, we did the best that we could.

In early summer of 2017, Robin and Isabelle were on their way to yoga when they came upon a litter of kittens running loose in the street. A tiny shape darted across the road, quickly followed by a second. They spotted a third in the grass on the side of the street, getting ready to pounce. The stopped the car to move the kittens to safety and to determine if these were loose pets, or strays.

They located five kittens, and it was easy to conclude that they did not have a caregiver and were at risk. Based on their sizes, they likely came from two separate litters, but the mother cats were nowhere to be found. One of them might have been ten weeks old at best, and the other four were six weeks

Not even old enough to be properly weened and with no mother in sight, Robin did what she normally does when she finds stray kittens and became their mother. She and Isabelle scooped up four of the little balls of fluff, and Isabelle was corralling them in the car when Robin went back to capture the fifth one.

She was carrying it back to the car when she looked down and saw a sixth kitten laying on its back. It was wedged into a crack in the pavement and was so small that it almost disappeared into the crevasse that was barely an inch deep. It was, unfortunately, deceased. It was a hot day out and it was likely that it had simply succumbed to the heat and dehydration. Robin handed the fifth kitten to Isabelle and then went back to retrieve the kitten that had passed away. She was going to bring him home and give him a proper burial. She was already crying as she shooed away the flies that were covering it and cradled it in her arms as she walked back to the car.

And then the dead kitten opened his eyes.

He was the smallest of the six, no more than four weeks old. He would certainly have passed away if Robin had not gathered him up.

Robin and Isabelle spent the rest of the day bathing each of the kittens and carefully brushing them and removing every single flea from their fur. When I came home from work later that day, they had already set up a cozy cave for them inside a large kennel in the basement. Three or four seemed to be in good shape, but there were a couple of them that we did not think would make it.

Isabelle named the litter after superheroes, so we had a Diana, a Natasha, a Felicity, a Loki, and an Odin. The smallest of the litter, the tiny orange kitten that we were afraid might pass away any moment, she named Thor. The god of thunder.

If ever there was a mismatched name, this had to be it. He looked more like a Thornton than a Thor, and he slept so much that we often referred to him as Thorazine. But as small as he was, his heart was mighty. He was the youngest and the smallest of the group, but he quickly became the most fearless as well. Or the most foolish. Robin has pointed out to me on numerous occasions that there is often little difference between the two.

We had initially thought he might pass away from simply being too little to sustain life. Even after we nursed him back to health, we were still concerned that he might not live long because he did not seem to understand what caution was or what was physically possible. If he was on the bed and wanted to be up on the kennel, he would simply launch himself off of the bed. There was no calculation or thought involved in it. No belief that all three inches of him would be able to complete a leap of several feet. He just did it.

We had to constantly watch him and even when he became big enough to wander about, he still could never be left outside the kennel on his own. He would decide that he wanted to be up on the entertainment console and would leap at it, regardless of the fact that his vertical jump amounted to less than six inches at the time and the console was three feet off the ground. He would just do it and if he failed, he would just do it again.

And it was not surprising that even though he was the smallest of the bunch, he was the first one to eventually successfully make the leap.

As part of his spirit of fearless exploration, he was also the first of the kittens that climbed the stairs to the second floor. This also meant that he was the first to encounter the "Door of Doom" behind which the resident cats had certainly informed him that a ferocious beast lurked. The ferocious beast immediately made his presence known and hissed at the smell of new cat that wafted under the door. Thor did not even flinch. Perhaps he truly was fearless, or perhaps, as most young of any species are, he lacked a proper understanding of mortality. Regardless of which force was motivating him, he approached the door and then looked up at me expectantly.

I am an analyst by profession, but I live my life much more instinctually. My instincts said that there was something in the energy here that had potential. Robin was not home at the time, which is when I make most of my foolish decisions, so I decided to open the door just the tiniest crack to see how the two reacted.

This was a delicate procedure. I had attempted the door crack introduction previously with other cats with disastrous results. No Tail had not extended his nose into the crack to sniff the cat on the other side on those occasions. He had shoved his arm into the crack and attempted to rip the door out of my hands and possibly off its hinges. Thor was also still very small and could likely squeeze through the tiniest opening so if I was going to attempt this, I had to be deliberate about the execution.

I leaned against the wall next to the door, putting the entire weight of my body into it. I then grabbed the door knob with one hand while bracing my elbow against the jamb, and grabbed my wrist with the opposite hand so that, theoretically, I could control how far the door opened and resist any efforts to push or pull it further. Carefully, ever so carefully, I turned the knob and slivered the door open the width of a kitten's nose.

Thor leaned in as the howls erupted from inside the room, and No Tail launched himself at the door. The opening, however, was so small that he could not get his mouth or his paws through the crack. It was not so small that Thor could not get his paw through. Standing the width of the door away from a frothing beast, Thor reached his tiny paw through the crack and bopped No Tail on his nose.

It was like he had hit the off switch. No Tail immediately stopped howling. He looked up at me through the crack in the door with a confused look on his face.

Did – did someone just…slap me?

Thor looked up at me expectantly. The analytical side of me said six ounces of kitten versus twelve pounds of furry dragon was not a good formula. The instinct side overruled the analyst and said, this is your chance.

I opened the door wide enough for the tiny orange adventurer to enter, and without hesitation he did. I was prepared to intervene at the expense of all of my exposed flesh, and for a moment I thought I would have to. No Tail reared up once again and stalked forward but before he could cover two steps, Thor stepped up to him once again, swatted him on the nose, and then walked away and began exploring the room.

I think that it was the utter insouciance that disconcerted No Tail. The swats from Thor weren't exactly playful but they definitely weren't aggressive. They were curious. Like any little kid pushing a button and wondering, "What does this do?"

When it failed to do anything interesting, he simply walked away and began checking out the new space that he had not previously seen. No Tail followed him for a moment or two, hulking over him and occasionally hissing, but Thor was more interested in seeing what toys No Tail had in his room. It was as if the nerdy kid had just walked into the living room of the school bully, and when the bully threatened him, he asks if he has any fun games to play on his computer.

No Tail was not only confused by Thor's actions, but he was also a bit offended by him. How dare this new kid not be terrified. That is not how these things were supposed to work. But it was too late. There was nothing to be done about it. Thor had discovered No Tail's water dish, and Thor loved playing in water.

11

I have a few theories about No Tail's reaction to Thor. It goes much deeper than Thor not being afraid. Other cats had stood up to No Tail before and he had not hesitated to attack, so that couldn't be it. I also don't think it was simply a matter of Thor being so tiny or young. I think those were only associative elements of the deeper reason.

I think that it had to do with innocence.

On the few occasions that I saw No Tail descend into his state of maddened rage, it always ended with a look of confusion and fear on his face, as if he had frightened himself with his own loss of control. Even as an animal, there was something about it that felt unnatural to him. He was okay with killing when killing was necessary, but not okay with the thing that lived inside him that smiled at the thought of death.

Whatever moral compass he had that had somehow managed to survive being broken by all of his traumas, still pointed true. There was an understanding of right and wrong. And perhaps like a certain soldier, he still needed some justification for his violence, however weak that justification might be. When faced with a kitten that was still unstained by any of the dark emotions that would justify his rage, he was conflicted. The toothed thing inside him wanted to act, but the part of No Tail that was still authentically and unconquerably him understood that it would be wrong. The righteous overcame the rage.

Perhaps allowing that part of him a moment of control gave him the ability to exercise discernment in his interactions with those where the distinction between innocence and shadow was less clearly defined.

I think that the recognition of innocence also plays a big part in why we are often driven to try to connect to animals, and why we are fascinated and compelled by those stories we see where a person makes a connection to a wild animal. Not everyone, but certainly a large percentage of people will attempt to speak to any new pets that they meet at a friend's house or while out on a walk. The impulse is so strong that service animals wear vests requesting that people not try and pet the animal. The warning is necessary because the assumption is that we will.

If you are an animal person, you will probably acknowledge that there is even an unspoken competition present anytime you enter a room with an animal in it to be the one that the animal "chooses." I have seen adults gloat when a dog chooses to sit next to them instead of another guest, and I have seen children glow when a cat decides to curl up in their lap.

When it is a stray or a wild animal, the encounters become even more full of awe. Popular culture is full of novels and movies about people befriending wild animals. We may have even spent time ourselves watching videos of people interacting with animals that seem so unbelievable, they border on magic.

There are entire mythologies built around these relationships, and often at their core is the social concept of innocence. One of the most popular of course is the idea that unicorns will only visit women of a "chaste and pure heart." I don't believe that you have to be a virgin to see fantastic creatures, but I do believe that we have a very broad understanding that animals have the ability to see inside a person's heart.

This creates both hope and fear. It all depends on what we think is in our heart.

When that deer or that squirrel or that magpie comes up to us though, we suddenly feel forgiven. We feel like maybe the good that we hope was in there is actually there.

Most of us are damaged in one way or another. Perhaps it comes from trauma we experienced. Perhaps it comes from trauma we inflicted. Perhaps trauma has nothing to do with it but we are simply like the majority of the teeming masses out there, running to and fro with our heads down and questioning our self-worth because of outlandish expectations that we may have allowed others to foist upon us, although more often than not they are expectations that we have piled upon ourselves until we feel we are about to collapse under the weight of our own inadequacies.

The world is so full of judgments that it can seem impossible to escape it, but then, a stray dog comes up to you, timidly at first, but then with increasing excitement it sniffs your hand and licks you, and suddenly you know that you can't be as bad as you thought you were, because the dog could see inside of you and still found you worth greeting.

I think that is why some people are drawn so strongly to rescue. We feel irredeemable and we are desperately begging the universe to send an animal our way because if that deer or raccoon or blue jay comes up to us, it means that they saw inside our heart and found something that was still untouched and clean, and maybe they don't see the blood on our hands.

I believe that this may even be the case with some animals. An animal that has the ability to understand right and wrong, and believes that they have acted on the dark side of that line too often may need to feel that acceptance the same as any human does.

And that is what I think walked in the door that day. It wasn't just Thor. It was innocence. And when innocence said that it saw what was inside No Tail and was not afraid of it, I think No Tail began to feel like he was worthy of letting go of his anger.

I am a rational adult, and when an animal at The Manor comes up to me even today, I still feel like the universe is sending me a magical message and letting me know that I have value and am not as damaged as I think. I think though, that one of the reasons that I loved No Tail so much was that he saw the blood on my hands and loved me anyway.

III

The change wasn't instant, but it was close to it. Thor excitedly trotted up the stairs every day to see his new best friend, and No Tail allowed him in, alternating between glaring at Thor in anger and staring up at me in confusion. I just looked back at him and shrugged.

Soon, the growling at the door stopped, and after a few days, Salem followed Thor into No Tail's room. Salem might have looked like a panther, but he was always just a big kid at heart and had enjoyed hanging out with the new kittens. He was probably as excited as Thor was to see what toys the new kid had in his room. By the time Luna came up to see his apartment, No Tail practically rolled his eyes at me and declared that this final indignity was simply too much. Shortly after that, we opened the door to let No Tail out in the evening without putting the other cats away, and from that point on the door remained open.

He was free to roam wherever he wanted to go and interact with the other cats, but he still wasn't fully integrated. He would eat with us and sleep in our bed and knock pieces off of the table during game nights, but he maintained a sense of aloofness. A separation from the other cats.

He did have occasional moments of bonding. At some point, Salem must have walked up to No Tail and said, "I hear you like bread. I too, like bread."

Then Salem showed No Tail the trick he had learned, where he would curl his paw around the round door knob on the pantry and pull it open. We were aware that Salem could do this, but Salem did not have No Tail's athletic prowess, so it had never been much of a concern for us. We simply moved the non-sealed food to the upper shelves and the problem was solved.

This solution had worked fine before No Tail and Salem were out at the same time, but our solution quickly fell apart when the two began to collaborate. The first time we came into the kitchen and found Salem sitting on the floor of the pantry, chewing through the plastic bag and eating the crust off of an entire loaf of bread, we assumed that the bag must have fallen. There was no way that Salem could have scaled the pantry shelves to acquire the prize. Salem, who had not had the sense to hide, just looked up at us and shrugged when we asked him how he had gotten the bread.

No Tail was suspiciously absent though, so we went searching. We found him under the bed in his room, busily devouring his own stolen slices.

We had an idea now of what must have happened, but we would not know the full extent of it for several days. The confirmation came later that week when we came down the stairs and peeked into the kitchen from the landing to see how everyone was getting along. What we saw was Salem doing his cat burglar trick with the doorknob, while No Tail waited patiently on the floor for him to open the pantry. Once that step was complete, No Tail went to work and parkoured his way eight feet up the shelves to grab the bag with the bread in it.

We foiled that plot, and began to put hair ties over the two doorknobs, to prevent them from being pulled open. This only slowed down the bread bandits. They discovered that if Salem pulled hard enough, he could create a gap big enough for No Tail to slip inside. Once inside, it was easier to push the door open far enough to provide access to anyone who wanted to join in the bread buffet. Eventually we were forced to purchase high-tension bungee cords to hold the doors closed and protect the English muffins and Irish scones from the Afghan invader.

This was not truly a friendship, however. It was a relationship of convenience. No Tail needed a partner, not a companion. His goal was still one of solitary intent. The emotional connection and the freedom to play would take longer.

IV

The ability to play is necessary to be truly free. This applies to cats as well as to children, and probably to adults as well, although most of us have likely forgotten that.

The importance of play was something that I learned back when Captain Nabil was still prowling the streets of Baqubah. Play is mostly instinctual. People and animals just do it. Developmentally though, play can be encouraged or discouraged. Perhaps if you are a kitten that has to fend for itself on the streets of Kabul, when you should still be nursing, or maybe a kid that sits by himself, reading literature when the rest of the kids are coloring pictures of otters, you don't really learn how to play properly.

The reason that play is important in exercising freedom, is that play develops creative pathways in the brain. Whether it is imagining a stick is a sword, or pretending a blanket is a fort, or simply pretending that a doll can talk, play gives a child the tool to see a thing that is and imagine a thing that is not. Without that ability, all we can ever be or do is confined by whatever our current state happens to be. And decisions made with limited information can never truly be a free decision.

If you are given potatoes and carrots for dinner every night and have never even heard the word pizza, and someone sets potatoes and carrots in front of you and asks you what you would like to eat for dinner, you are going to choose potatoes or carrots. You are literally incapable of doing anything else. If no one ever told you that there even was such a thing as pizza or tacos, you are never going to choose anything but potatoes and carrots. There could be an entire buffet of pizza and tacos just around the corner but if you don't know it exists, potatoes and carrots is what you are going to have. To call it a choice would be partially true, but it wouldn't be the complete truth.

No Tail had been de-murderized by Thor, but his interactions with the other cats, and with his people was still very limited. It wasn't real freedom because he still didn't understand what choices were available to him. Before Thor, his choices, when presented with another cat was to kill them. So basically, his freewill package wasn't even up to the pre-cable, coat-hanger antenna version of choice. After Thor, his choices had been expanded by one. He could still choose to kill, which he thankfully did not, but his only other option was "not to kill," which was definitely a broad category but far from exclusive. So, when he chose non-violence, it was a limited choice option. He wasn't "choosing" non-violence. He was simply choosing not to do the violence, which is not quite the same thing.

When he saw the other cats play, he would watch them, but he would never join in. If a cat could sneer with disdain, No Tail would definitely have been sneering as he observed them. It was clear that he thought they were stupid, chasing their fake birds and plush mousies and sparkly foam balls around the room. No Tail was more worldly. He knew the toys weren't real. Clearly the other cats were being silly, acting like they were actually attacking something. He would stand to the side and observe them and roll his eyes. He reminded me of the young girl in "Miracle on 34th Street" who thought other children were foolish for playing make believe.

Enter Salem and Eliza.

Salem was the epitome of a house panther. His head and body looked like someone had taken a shrink ray and directed it onto a full-sized panther in order to shrink him down to fun size. At almost thirteen pounds though, he still had the impressive look of a predator that was able to dispatch a fleeing gazelle.

That is, until he smiled at you and started playing. He went from "regal predator of the plains" to "doofy" in the time it took for him to sink his fangs into the nearest cardboard box. The glorious thing about Salem was that he was about as unselfconscious as a cat could possibly be. He gave zero meows about what other people or animals thought about him. He could not be bothered with your opinion of him. He was too busy enjoying life.

The second feline influence was a lithe little ballerina of a kitten that walked into our house one day not too long after Thor arrived. And I do mean it literally when I say that she walked in.

We occasionally had stray cats show up on our back porch that we would take in to one of the rescue groups that we worked with to be adopted out if possible, or TNR'd if not. Sometimes it was necessary to catch them in one of our live traps, but we had developed an alternative trapping method that seemed to work just as well. When a cat became accustomed to eating on the back porch, we would put the other cats away, place a dish of food inside our house, and then open the sliding glass door.

Prior to opening the door, we would attach a rope to the door handle and then one of us would position ourselves in the kitchen to observe. When the stray came inside to eat the food, we would pull the rope, sliding the door closed and trapping the new cat inside. Eliza was less than six months old when we slid the door closed behind her.

She was shy at first, but Isabelle used the same cage technique she had used on Jack, and soon she had the run of the house. She was as goofy as Salem was, and just as playful. It was impossible for a cat to live in the same house as them and not become infected to some degree with their sense of carefree joie de vivre.

Over time, No Tail's look of isolation began to soften. It became less aloof, and less haughty. It began to be replaced by a look of longing. Watching him stand to the side, it was no longer disdain that he projected, but a desire to join in. He just didn't know how.

We would encourage him. Verbally, we would reassure him that it was okay to play with the other cats and to have fun with the toys, and physically we would try to entice him by tossing fluff mouses his way or pulling a string past where he lay on the carpet. He would look at these toys the way someone might look at a piece of chewed gum that someone set down on a chair next to them.

Finally, in 2018, two and a half years after he had come home, we were playing with three of the other cats in the breakfast room. The toy that we were using was a fake bird on a string that would make a sound similar to a bird flapping its wings when you spun it around. The other two were taking turns attacking it in the air, and we would also drag it across the floor so that Luna could pretend to attack it as well, since she is more of a ground predator. As the bird spun around the room and whipped toward the edge of the sofa, a black streak came out of nowhere, grabbed the bird in its mouth, and disappeared into the shadows.

We all looked at each other in shock and amazement, even the other cats. Almost immediately No Tail emerged from beneath the sofa and looked around with wide eyes as if he too was not quite sure what had just happened. Then he stalked off, embarrassed like he had just asked the popular girl at the prom to dance with him and she had turned him down.

We tried to entice him back into the room, but he not only left the room, he actually went upstairs to his old room and sat down on the bed. It is likely that he was as unequipped to handle the new emotion that he had felt when he had tried to join in playing with the other cats as he had been by Thor's refusal to act afraid. It was outside of his frame of reference. For days afterward, he kept to himself.

No Tail was always a deep thinker. Even when he had been more consumed with rage, he was still thoughtful about it. New experiences did not simply generate reactions in him. They generated a deliberate mental process where he considered what had been before, what new thing he had encountered, and how he would react to that new thing in the future.

After processing his attempt at playing for about a week, he made a second foray into the world of make believe. It was as unexpected as the first, but it was less fleeting than the first encounter had been. He made several passes at the toy that we had been playing with before finally deciding to walk away.

His style of play was blatantly more violent than that of the other cats. It would sometimes come across more as a martial arts training video than an image of a cat at play. There was still a lot of anger in him. It had not disappeared when he stopped attacking the other cats. He had simply learned to control it, and when he attacked the toys, he allowed much of the fevered, violent joy to direct his actions. Replacements were required on a regular basis now and we would buy back up birds and balls in bulk.

We also learned that once he got energized in the pursuit of a toy, it was necessary to carefully supervise the involvement with the other cats. Once his predator mode was activated, he struggled to distinguish the difference between attacking a wind-up mouse and attacking another cat. There was a time or two when he mashed down on the kill switch too hard and flipped back into murder mode for a moment, and physical intervention was necessary, and a cool down period of separation was required, but most of his negative interactions with the rest of the clowder settled down into the more mundane types of physical violations that you might typically see among siblings.

We were overjoyed. Finally, he was beginning to relax and enjoy life.

The joy of the breakthrough into the discovery of play, however, was short-lived as he began to experience a rapid loss of weight, and as quickly as his play had developed, his activity level began to decrease. In cats, particularly those that were once feral, that's a one-two punch. Loss of weight and loss of activity are often precursors to a worst-case scenario. We thought at first that his reduction in activity might simply be a behavioral issue, since previously his greatest activity of interest was violence, but it quickly became apparent that letting go of rage and finding some peace at last in his life was not the source of his malaise. The vet would soon confirm this suspicion.

So as No Tail began to let go of his anger, I fixated on his loss of health and grasped onto my rage with both hands, determined to make someone or something pay, but it was just another excuse. Somewhere around the first time that I ever held a dead child in my arms was about the time that I began to use righteousness as an excuse for rage instead of the reason for it.

V

Abbas was five or six when I first met him. I can't remember exactly. There is a lot about that incident that I can't remember. Sometimes the connections get crossed, and I find myself recalling the event from completely different perspectives. In one memory, I am the soldier, sitting there on the ground, looking down at this dead child in my arms. In another memory, I am just a spectator, looking at this soldier who is sitting on the ground, holding a dead child in his arms. The tableau is a bit like the picta, except in my version Mary is wearing body armor, and Jesus never made it past his sixth birthday. Or fifth. Like I said, I can't remember exactly.

The one thing that I do recall is that he wasn't wearing shoes. When you are faced with unspeakable horror, which let's just call it what it is, anytime a five or six year old child has been executed is pretty horrible, and yet here we are speaking about it, so maybe unspeakable isn't the best term for it. The reason I remember the shoes is because my driver was the one that had bought shoes for him.

Abbas had become something like a mascot for our team. His father was a cab driver and would occasionally do odd jobs for us. When I might need to go somewhere that required something less obtrusive than a soldier in uniform pulling up in a Humvee, he was the one that would drive me.

Abbas went everywhere with him, and getting a chance to interact with a playful child was a much needed break for our team since we spent most of our days engaged in past times that only the emotionally damaged would call playful. We would give him candy whenever we could, and small toys that we had sent to us or that we hand-selected from the many boxes we received from the toy drive that we organized.

The shoes was the thing that stuck with me though. A lot of kids run around without shoes, no matter where you live. I had spent a large part of my youth running barefoot through the yard and pulling out the devil's head thorns that would draw blood and occasional tears from me, but never a commitment to wear my shoes the next time I went outside. Abbas was no different than any five year old. Or six year old.

Our driver was able to get his shoe size though and purchased a pair for him. He really liked those shoes. He wore them everywhere after that and would show off his new shoes to anyone who would listen. I think it was more that they were a gift, and less about the shoes themselves. He was proud of them, but I think he was more proud that he had someone that cared enough about him to buy him new shoes. Not that he would have likely been able to explain it in that manner, or even process it internally at his age.

And in return, I repaid his excitement by getting him killed.

I know, I know. CRT, right? I was paying attention. I wrote it down. I reframed the trauma. It wasn't my fault. I wasn't the one that shot him.

I have spent countless hours in therapy telling my therapist that it wasn't my fault, and I have a degree in this psychology stuff, so I am aware that what I am doing is internalizing an external incident and assigning blame to myself for the actions of another person that I could not control.

On paper that all makes sense. At two in the morning though, when the shadows point their fingers at me, all I know is that I could not protect an innocent child.

The world began to slip out of its orbit around reason at that moment. The weight of darkness held a much greater gravitational pull than the weight of reason. The fire that had been a sanctified flame inside me, whose purpose had been to light the way in the darkness began to grow. And when a fire grows, it must be fed. The paschal flame spilled out of its brazier and began to demand to be fed.

The problem with fire is that it is never satisfied. If it does not eat, it dies. It also is not discerning, so it does not care what it eats. You can feed it anything. Your emotions. Your relationships. Your sanity. It will still want more. You can chuck yourself and everyone around you into it and it will still continue to whisper to you, "More, give me more," until you become nothing but a dry husk of sorrow filled with a fire that desperately wants you to break apart so that its sparks can find other souls to burn.

Before, injustice had been the focus, and rage was just the tool that I happened to use to attack the problem. Now it was the rage that was the focus, and injustice was the convenient tool that allowed me attack.

VI

In the spring of 2018, I retired from my military career, and the fire department would wind up being called to our house for the second time.

The first time had been six months earlier. My younger daughter had competed in a cardboard boat competition at the University of Kansas, and she and I had built a craft to be proud of. We had taken several of the heavy duty cardboard rolls that upholstery fabric is rolled on and had built a craft that was part outrigger, part next-generation hovercraft. It was so watertight and well designed that we could have sailed it to Fiji.

The KU boat race was much less demanding, requiring only that the craft traverse the pond next to the stadium on campus.

Once she had successfully completed the competition, however, we were left with a large and sturdy seacraft, but no sea. It was not something that lent itself to being scrap booked but we also could not bear the thought of simply throwing such a fine vessel into the dust bin. We decided instead that a boat worthy of a Viking was worthy of a Viking funeral.

We drove the boat home and placed it onto the new firepit I had built, but it was still wet from the race so I decided to augment its flammability with a small amount of gasoline. Then, because I had spent too much time with combat engineers, I decided to add a little more gas.

When we tossed the match onto the pyre to send our boat to Valhalla, the resulting explosion rattled windows and a fireball rose thirty feet into the air. We immediately realized that we might have overcalculate the amount of gasoline needed, and suspected that authorities might soon be involved so we turned on the hose and extinguished the blaze as quickly as we could.

In less than two minutes, we heard sirens. In five, they were in our neighborhood. There was still a thin stream of smoke rising up from the sodden ashes and half-burned cardboard but in the growing twilight, it was difficult to see. After ten minutes of driving slowly up and down the neighborhood to ensure that a meteor had not struck an ammo dump, the fire trucks finally drove away, unable to identify the source of the multiple alarmed calls they had received.

At my retirement party, it was an odor and not a sound that wound up bringing the men in yellow.

Near the conclusion of the party, when it was time for me to make my speech, I went into the house and returned moments later, in full uniform. Robin was surprised because when I had taken it off for the last time a month previously, I had sworn I would never put it back on again. She quickly realized my intent, however, when I climbed up on the edge of our stone fire pit and began to speak.

And strip.

I thanked everyone for coming and then began to take off each piece of my uniform. I would remove a piece of clothing, make a reference to a part of my career, then remove any insignia and present it to one of the people at the party. Once the piece of clothing had been relieved of its significance, it was cast into the fire.

Rank, unit patches, combat patches, tabs, nametapes, flags. They all came off and were presented to my friends and family, and hat, jacket, and pants were consigned to the flames. At last, I was standing there in nothing but my boxer shorts and my boots.

"It is sometimes said that the dirt of the place where blood has been shed will continue to call to you after you have left. For that reason, soldiers will often leave a pair of boots behind them in order to trick the ground into believing that they are still there. That way they can go away and live their lives in peace, without fear of being called back again.

I have left boots behind on too many occasions and yet I keep getting called back, again and again. Well, this time I have no intention of ever returning. This time, I am burning the boots. Let the blood-soaked dirt try and find these boots now."

And with that, I tossed them into the fire.

The cheers rose up as I stood there in my shorts, and then the smoke began to rise up. The uniform up until that point had all been fabric. It had simply burned up for the most part. The boots though had thick rubber soles, and once that started burning, it smelled like something with a giant red caution sign on it had just caught on fire.

It was annoying but I didn't realize that it was alarming until the alarms actually began to sound. This time it was easy for the fire trucks to spot the source of the disturbance, and as they came around the back of the house and saw me still standing on the rim of the firepit in my boxers, I am not sure what their first thoughts were, but they weren't great.

They at first cautioned me about lighting fires while inebriated but I assured them that I had not had any alcohol. Then they cautioned me about burning dangerous materials in an open flame. We explained to them that it was a retirement ceremony and that we had just been burning a uniform and had not realized how badly boots can smell when they are on fire. They finally let that one go, but then they started examining my firepit.

"City regulation says firepits have to be four feet wide or smaller," the fireman told me.

"This one is exactly four feet wide," I told him. "I built it myself."

The fireman eyed the pit suspiciously. "Are you sure that's only four feet?" he asked.

"Right at," I replied. "Built it myself."

I had no idea how wide it actually was of course. I was just relying on the same Jedi mind trick that had let me walk my dog into the Smithsonian, right in front of the security guard. As the fireman continued to stare at the pit however, it seemed it was more difficult to be a Jedi when you are standing in your boxers.

After a few more moments of staring, he finally let it go. We invited the fireman to stay and join the party, but they politely refused and returned to their station. I returned to the house to put on actual clothes.

No Tail was sitting in the window, watching the fire trucks depart. The sirens had scared away all of the other cats, but he seemed to enjoy the spectacle. He always did. During Independence Day celebrations, when fireworks turned our neighborhood into a sparkly, smoke-filled combat zone, with constant explosions from noon until midnight, he would sit in the upstairs window and watch.

With the flashing lights turned off, the trucks lost their interest for him and he came and sat down on the bed as I got dressed.

So you're retired now, he said. What's next? Are you finally going to relax? Or are you going to keep jumping into the fire?

And the truth was, I didn't know.

VII

In the fall of 2018, when No Tail began to rapidly lose weight, and his appetite started to decline. I took him in to the vet immediately to get checked out. We had always known that he had some gastro-intestinal issues because of his loose stools, and it was initially our hope that this was just a case of kitty flu or an upset tummy, but after multiple visits and different medicines and diet changes, it was not getting better.

By our third visit, we had progressed to x-rays and extensive blood work, as well as an internal biopsy. The results that came back were everyone's worst fears. No Tail had cancer.

We were all devastated. I have worked with strays enough to know that, although an outdoor cat's lifespan can be fifteen years or more, diseases and injuries impact those timelines so that ten or twelve years is rather common for them even after they have been brought inside.

No Tail was FIV positive, which in itself used to be considered a death sentence, and he had obviously had extensive previous injuries. At ten years old, it would not have been unusual for him to have passed away at that age. We accepted this as a possibility, but we began to explore our options.

Much like it is with people, the options are limited once the cancer is discovered. The choices are also much the same. Surgery, radiation, and chemotherapy. And as it is with people, those choices are hard to make.

If a person has cancer, they are not only part of the discussion, but they are usually the primary decision maker. They are able to process the emotional cost of the pain and the procedures and are able to engage in personal statistical modeling when discussing likely outcomes with the physician.

Animals do not have that option. When it is an animal, the burden of choice must be borne by the person.

I love math. It is a fun hobby of mine. Statistics and analysis are part of what I do. There is no formula though to answer the question of whether or not you should attempt to prolong someone's life. There is no "if pain is X and sorrow is Y and the time delta of mortality is represented by n, and the likelihood of a non-fatal outcome is .37, then the obvious choice is two rounds of chemo."

It is not simply a matter of variables. It is a matter of unknowns. And at the end of the day, our ability to communicate our choice to No Tail is limited. Our ability to understand his preference is almost non-existent.

The doctor explained that due to his FIV and his advanced age, and his decreased kidney function, he might not even survive the surgery, and attempting chemo or radiation treatment might make him so ill that he would stop eating altogether. A person can be ill from chemo but if you explain it to them and they understand there is a potential end in sight, they might be encouraged to eat and work to stay healthy, but an animal might simply feel like it is dying. Worse, it might think that it is being attacked and that we are the ones trying to kill it.

There was also the issue of cost.

Cost should never be part of a calculation when it comes to someone's life, but unfortunately it is. We were accustomed to spending hundreds of dollars on our pet's health, and we were well over a thousand in at this point with No Tail. We were in a position where we were prepared to spend thousands and even put ourselves into debt to save his life. The most aggressive treatments available however were not in the thousands. They were in the tens of thousands.

At that point in our lives, it was simply not an option. We did not have the money and we did not have the means to get it. If I had had twenty thousand available to me at the time, we might have chosen to pursue the combination of surgery and chemo and I would have moved to the town the hospital was in and spent my day with him as he underwent treatment.

With the options that were presented to us then at the time, we chose a treatment option that consisted mostly of "wait and see." If he continued to lose weight and began to look as if he were suffering, we would have to be prepared to step in and make that next difficult decision of euthanasia. So, we watched and waited and hoped that the cancer would just go away.

And against all odds, it did. His appetite picked back up and he put weight back on until he looked just like his old self. Within three months he was back to normal. The doctor was a bit surprised, but he said that sometimes cancer does go into remission on its own.

It was still there. The blood tests showed that his white blood cells were better, and the x rays showed that the mass in his GI tract had actually reduced in size, but it was still there. The only negative lasting effect seemed to be that his stools were now looser than before.

When we had brought No Tail home, I had gotten it into my mind for some reason that I needed him to live for at least five years. I'm not sure what calculations I used to arrive at that number, but it felt right in my head. He had lived outside and had had a rough life for the first seven years of his life. Somehow, I felt that if he lived inside in comfort and relative ease for five years, maybe it would start to erase some of those memories of pain and hardship and loneliness and going without that he had endured previously. I thought that when he passed away, which is a thing that is inevitable for all of us, that the pleasant memories would be what filled his mind, and his passing into whatever lay beyond would be more peaceful. Like maybe there would be a sense of completeness. My random compassion math had determined that five years of love were necessary to counterbalance seven years of pain and neglect.

I wonder what it was inside myself that I was trying to balance out and compensate for. I wonder how much that math drives my day to day actions. Do I try to do things for others because I am desperately wanting to be loved to make up for my own years of loneliness? Do I work hard to earn a lifestyle of ease so that I can somehow reassure that little homeless six year old inside me that things are actually better? Do I feel a need to make the world a better place so that when I too am ready to pass away that I can do it with a degree of peace and a modicum of hope that something better is coming?

I think a lot of that thinking goes into the psychology of a bucket list. Things that we feel we must do or feel in order for us to feel like our time here mattered. Things that are necessary so that we do not feel like our lives were wasted because the bad so overshadowed the good that what was even the point of it all.

I think that is one of the reasons that some religions paint such an extreme image of what the afterlife is like. Inherently they know that life is full of suffering and so an afterlife is created that is so full of peace and joy that all suffering can be endured for the sake of what comes.

I think that a focus on the afterlife does a disservice to ourselves and those around us. Not enough effort is put into ending suffering here, because what does it matter if we suffer for the mere pittance which is a human lifespan in relation to an eternity of joy and excess? I think that it is important that we seek some form of balance while we are alive. If we would pass with peace and acceptance, the positive end of the see-saw shouldn't be on the other side. The imbalance between suffering and love should not be so great that it takes an eternity of golden mansions to equal our seventy or eighty years of pain on earth.

Which is the long way of repeating that I had determined in my mind that No Tail deserved to live at least five years with us to make up for the previous seven years of his life. If he lived that long, then my anger at the imbalance in the universe would be mitigated. Somewhere in my mind there was a score card, and the universe was way behind on points for goodness and justice.

And maybe that's where it came from. Maybe it wasn't five years to make No Tail's life balanced. Maybe I was just being selfish. In fact, I'm certain I was being selfish. No Tail deserved those five years, but it was me that NEEDED those five years. For the five year old me that lived in a tent and ate out of date canned goods and for the five year old Iraqi boy that I held after he was executed by terrorists and for the five year old girl that was shot by guards at an American check point because no one spoke the same language, I needed those five years so that there would not be this cosmic imbalance of darkness when it was my turn to pass on.

And somehow the universe obliged. No Tail began to gain some of his weight back, and his usual energy levels returned.

I think it had more to do with No Tail's nature though than it did with a sentient universe acknowledging that it owed me something. That character that had made him continue living when he had been injured five or six years earlier and had forced him to go on even with broken legs, when most other animals or even people would have quit somehow kept him going.

It was a year before he suffered his next big setback. He began to lose weight again and his appetite reduced, and his stools became looser. This time though, we knew what we were dealing with. We went in to our vet and exams were conducted. By now, our finances were a little bit healthier, and we discussed more extreme options.

The vet this time advised against taking any further measures. His opinion was that the likelihood of success did not justify the increased suffering that we would have to put No Tail through. His advice at that time was to simply make his life as comfortable as possible and keep an eye on him for that inevitable moment when the suffering became too great.

"How much time?' I asked him. I knew this was a foolish question. I knew that he didn't have a crystal ball and that he wasn't going to give me a definitive answer.

"Once the decline begins, it could be a matter of days. Perhaps even hours."

"When will that be?" I pushed.

"It's hard to say," he replied. He wasn't avoiding the question. He was trying to be kind.

"A week?" I asked.

"He doesn't look like he is on the verge of rapid decline right now so there's no reason to think that he only has a week left."

"A month?" I asked.

"I think that he will probably make it a month. Could be more."

"Six months?" I asked.

"That's…a possibility," he said, more slowly this time.

"Would it be reasonable to expect him to live a year?" I asked.

He didn't respond at first, which was answer enough for me. He just shook his head, and I could tell that he was struggling to answer the question. When I refused to break eye contact however, he finally answered me.

"I think that would be unlikely. I think that you should take it a day at a time and enjoy the time you have with him. If he is still with us in six months, we would be lucky, and we should be thankful for that."

I nodded. That was all I could do. I couldn't speak at first, and when I did all I could manage was another nod and an "Okay." I probably repeated that word a half a dozen times before I felt capable of attempting any other conversation without falling into tears.

A year would come and go, and No Tail would not be the first of our clowder that we said farewell to.

VIII

The Pirate showed up at our back door in 2019. He did not have a peg leg or a cutlass in his teeth, and the nearest body of water was the Missouri River, but there was little doubt in our minds that the tuxedo cat that strolled through our yard that late winter, when there was still snow on the ground, was a pirate. His swagger emphasized the "Jolly" in Jolly Roger, but the skull and crossbones was also clearly part of his DNA.

Thor and Salem were enamored of him. They would come to the back door and watch him climb the stairs to the deck and command the backyard as if he were a captain surveying the sea from his forecastle. A third member of our household though, fell truly and deeply, head over heels in love with him.

Robin.

She would scan the yard for him every day, as faithfully as any eighteenth century sea captain's wife, walking the widow's walk and staring out to sea, hoping for any sign of his sail on the horizon. It was not long before she would sit out on the deck and wait for him, and every day he would come closer and closer. He would eat the food that we left out for him, and would even eat in our presence, but he was not taken in by the sliding door trick. We put out live traps to catch him so that we could bring him in to get checked out, but he scoffed at our feeble attempts to tame him. This cat belonged to the open seas.

The Pirate's name was O'Malley.

A few months after first spotting the tuxedo scalawag, he showed up at our back door looking unwell. There was something wrong with his mouth. He was drooling excessively and even from a distance we could see that his gums were inflamed, and his jaw was swollen. We assumed it was either poison or a broken jaw, but either way it was obvious to us that we had no time to delay. We had to catch him right away.

Our first attempt ended in a dismal failure, and O'Malley ran from the yard. We thought that would be the last we would see of him. It was clear that he had come to us because he was injured, but stray cats view capture attempts as attacks, so we thought we had wasted what little trust value that we held with him. Two days later though, he returned. His condition was worsening, and whether he was weakened or whether he was willing, our second attempt succeeded, and we brought O'Malley, the Pirate to our veterinarian in Blue Springs.

The diagnosis was serious but not terminal. O'Malley had stomatitis which is a condition in which a cat's body develops what amounts to an allergic reaction to their own teeth. Untreated, it is fatal, but treated it has a fair chance of long-term success. O'Malley quickly became our most expensive cat ever, but his condition was brought under control, and he became the newest member of the Krasnesky Clowder.

I was concerned about how No Tail would react to O'Malley when we finally integrated him. All of our rescues had their own traumas and their own challenges, but O'Malley was the only one that had "street cat" energy. He had plenty of scars of his own, and although I recalled the way No Tail had put Monster to flight when they had fought, I suspected that O'Malley might be up to the task if a conflict arose.

O'Malley had a much more nonchalant approach to violence though. There was always a sense of cheerfulness about him. Like he would not hesitate to sink your ship, but he just might be singing the score from "Pirates of Penzance" while he did it. He also had a style of fighting that I had never seen in a cat before. O'Malley was a boxer.

It is impossible to describe, so you will just have to take our word for it. He had these huge anchors of fists for paws. When we had first seen him in the backyard, we had thought that he was a polydactyl. A cat with more than the normal number of toes. When he came inside, we realized that his paws had the regular number of toes. He simply had massive paws.

He used them to great effect. I know. I was the recipient of more than a few of his punches in the early days. On the few occasions that we saw him fight with other cats, he would snap out one of those massive fists and knock the other cat to the ground. When he and Jack scrapped a little less than playfully one time, O'Malley knocked him down so hard that I was worried Jack might have gotten a little kitty concussion. O'Malley had no need to bare his claws when he had the ability to just knock out his opponent.

No Tail and O'Malley did not immediately become best friends and bond over their past traumas, but neither did they become mortal enemies and destroy the house around them as they battled, which they were probably capable of doing. O'Malley did provide an important alternative approach to life for No Tail though. He had the potential for violence, but there was no rage inside him. No hate that was eating him up. Violence was only a tool, and unless it was needed, it stayed tucked away in his toolbox. There were too many other tools in the box to limit yourself to just one.

O'Malley sailed into his new life as an indoor cat with all of his sails unfurled. Full speed ahead! He became Robin's constant companion, following her around the house as faithfully as the most noble golden retriever. O'Malley was not reserved with his love, and showed affection for everyone, but the complete abandonment of self and unconditional love that he showered upon Robin was rare in any species, and it was beautiful just to be able to observe it.

And eventually he and No Tail did become best friends. Perhaps it was the traumas. Perhaps they bonded over their prior times as outdoor strays. Maybe they just liked the same types of music, but whatever the reason, it was only a matter of months before we would come into the room and find the two of them, curled up together on the big, gold salon chair.

The stomatitis though had not gone away. It was constantly being treated and it eventually led to O'Malley needing to have all of his teeth surgically removed. One of the problems with conditions that cause constant inflammation and tissue damage is that it often presents an increased risk of cancer. After a year of constant surgeries and infections, that is what happened.

2020 was a difficult year for the clowder. Breve, our oldest cat was suffering from kidney issues, which is common in elderly cats. Breve passed away early that year after the natural progression of his condition worsened.

Later that year, the Pirate's cancer began to rapidly advance, and by that fall he was gone.

With two recent losses hanging over our heads, we received a third blow when we took Salem in for his regular checkup, and to have a small bump on his head checked out to see if it might be a cyst. It turned out to be brain cancer, and our doofy, carefree boy began to be impacted by the spreading tumor. He crossed over before the cancer could remove the shine from his toothy grin.

And No Tail. The one that would be lucky to live another six months?

Inexplicably, he went into another round of remission and recovered. He would never regain his full weight again, but his energy level and his enjoyment of life were undiminished.

This is where some people would remark that life is funny sometimes. The one that you think is going to die doesn't, and the ones that weren't supposed to die do. But it's not really funny, is it? When people say that, I think that at best what they mean is that life is odd and unpredictable. The underlying reality is a lot more frightening. It isn't funny. It isn't odd. It is terrifyingly random.

Rescuing cats that are high-risk is a lot like combat, which is also a high-risk activity. It hints at being reasonable. It teases you with it. It makes just enough sense so that when it stops making sense it has the power to knock you off of your feet.

The first time I went to war, I was quickly disabused of the notion of logic and sense. I think that is why I so quickly and completely embraced the concept of chaos theory. Simple systems that flirt with predictability suddenly show themselves to be far more complex and susceptible to imperceptible changes so that attempting any kind of projections become pointless.

One grenade kills three soldiers, while another one thrown at you breaks apart at your feet. A kid picks up a dud round that goes off and kills him, but you wander through a field that you only find out afterwards is mined. A friend drives off base one time to do a health check and is killed by an IED, but when you respond to an IED report and are sent the wrong coordinates and park literally on top of the IED it fails to go off, even though you capture the guy that set it and he is mad because he is certain that he did it right, and EOD checks out the connections afterwards and can find no reason that it did not blow you sky high when the bomber kept pressing the detonation button over and over and over again, and how on earth is any of that fair or make any sense at all?!

During my second deployment was when I first began to actively seek out chaos and disreason. There was no benefit to playing it safe. No juice in it. No vig on the investment.

Life made no sense, and so in a senseless world, it made perfect sense that the cat who was supposed to die was the one that lived. After all, I was still here too. No Tail and I were bonded in rage and now we were also bonded in living past what reason would have dictated was our expiration date. The list of those that preceded us would soon grow even longer.

IX

In May of 2021, the United States began its withdrawal from Afghanistan. Those of us in the intel world knew that the collapse of the sitting Afghan government was all but inevitable, but even we were surprised by how quickly it all fell.

I say "we", but by 2021 I had been out of uniform for two years. I was no longer an intelligence officer. I had traded my battle dress uniform and combat boots for custom made suits and leather wingtips. Working as a financial advisor, I spent my days at a desk, analyzing market trends instead of terrorist activity, and buying and selling stocks instead of information. The news though made my recently vacated life suddenly alive again, and I started making calls.

It was soon clear that my ability to intervene in any positive manner was practically non-existent. The kids that we had given chess sets to, in defiance of the base commander in 2015, were now going to be under the rule of a government that had previously outlawed chess because they viewed the pieces as idols. Dina, the ten-year-old girl that I had purchased scarves from in the street on the way to meetings with provincial leaders, would now grow up under the authority of men who were intent on returning her and all of the girls of Afghanistan to lives of servitude.

With no other outlet, I began to fixate on the only avenue where I felt like I might be able to make a difference. The animals and the people of Now Zad.

The organization that had saved No Tail and brought him home to me was still in Kabul. Its staff and its animals were trapped there as the enemy combatants began to flood into the city.

Pen Farthing, the Royal British Commando who had founded Now Zad began broadcasting video from inside their compound in Kabul. They had originally been able to set up a flight to get everyone out but the British government had denied their flight plan, so now they were stuck.

For the next week, I spent most of my time trying to find a way to get them out of Afghanistan. Because of the time differences between here and the UK and Afghanistan, I did not sleep much. I made calls to Now Zad to see how we could help. I called British politicians. I called local news stations, and No Tail even got his own interview with a Kansas City station as we tried to drum up awareness of the plight of these vulnerable rescuers and animals.

No Tail stayed with me the entire time. Whether it was two in the morning and I was trying to get a call through to a representative at the airport in Kabul or two in the afternoon while I was on the phone to an animal rescue in Vegas, seeing if we could somehow borrow the jet from the owner of the Las Vegas Raiders, No Tail never left my side. He knew that I was stressed, but it was more than that. Somehow he knew what it was all about. He understood it had to do with him and with the people back where he had come from.

I had already started looking at flights into London. I knew that I wasn't really going to do it. I wasn't going to fly to London and get on the plane to Kabul and fly back to Afghanistan. Not really. But I wanted to make sure that I had everything in place so that if I did decide to act impulsively, my spur of the moment actions wouldn't need any additional planning.

Robin has known me a long time though. When she came down into the basement and saw my papers and diagrams spread out everywhere, and the look on my face after staying up for days on end, trying to save some stray animals half a world away, she didn't hesitate.

"You are not going back to Afghanistan."

I mustered up my best confused luck, and said, "I am just talking to people and trying to help," as if the thought of going myself had never crossed my mind.

She knew that my response was my legal response. It was not a denial. She was not going to let me get away with that.

"I want to hear you say it," she said.

I paused. I knew what she wanted me to say and I knew that I didn't want to say it. Regardless of how unlikely it was that I would ever actually follow through on it, but if I said it, I couldn't go back on it. That chance would be gone.

I tried making a joke out of it.

"That would be crazy," I said, and laughed. "Can you just see me getting off the plane in Kabul and commandeering a vehicle to get a bunch of cats?"

Robin did not laugh. She just waited.

"I will not go to Kabul and try to rescue the cats."

It caught in my throat as I said it, and there was no humor in the room. There was simply the anger of a person who had seen me put the need of play-acting the hero ahead of her needs and the needs of my family far too often. It wasn't cute. It wasn't endearing. It was self-destructive at best. At worst, it was self-centered.

Robin paused to stare at me for a moment and then shook her head and went back upstairs.

I sat down and petted No Tail for a moment. He looked up at me and let me know that Robin was right.

In the end, the Now Zad team and their animals made it out of Kabul without any assistance from No Tail or me. All we could do is watch in horror along with everyone else and do nothing. Time lost. Lives lost. But I at least had one consolation that not everyone else had. A broken little furry consolation that loved me.

Life moved on, and at the end of 2021, so would we.

No Tail Moves to the Manor

"The Lovin' Spoonful asked the same thing. Do I believe in magic? The Boss sang about it, didn't he? Kylie and Kate, hell, the damn Chairman of the Board himself sang about it," Lou said. "Olivia Newton John said we have to believe we ARE magic."

"That's music, not life," Ian said.

"Same thing," Lou replied. "Music IS life. And what did Queen say about it?"

"It's a kind of magic," Ian said, reluctantly.

"It's a kind of magic! Hallelujah, yes, he did say that, and we never question Freddie," Lou said in a reverent tone, placing his hand reassuringly on Ian's shoulder.

"You're mad," Ian said.

"I'm magical!" Lou replied.

FROM **"DEAD LETTER OFFICE"**, BY THAD KRASNESKY

SOLD

I

It was early September in 2021 when Robin received a text message from a friend.

"The Broadway house is for sale!"

That was all it said. Accompanying the text message was a link to a social media page where notable houses around the country were listed and featured.

Robin had been in love with the Broadway house since we had first moved to Kansas in 2011. It was the stuff of dreams. The type of house that promised secret rooms where you might still hear echoes of conversations between people decked in morning coats and pronouncing the "a" in "rather" like an "o". It was a place out of time, and if any of those stories we read as children, where magical doorways led into strange worlds or where mythical creatures wandered in the mists at the edge of the forest, had even a grain of truth to them, this was the house where those things just might happen. It was a house that looked imposing, but smelled like home, like a favorite grandparent. It simmered with the scents of candles on a dark night, warm fires on a snowy day, the dust of crunchy fall leaves, and something indescribable that we might call magic if we didn't know any better.

And Robin, as practical as she can be at times, had been utterly captivated by it. In appearance it is a three-story, red brick manor home with a fourth story attic, a captain's walk on the roof, multiple balconies, almost a hundred windows, and long curving drive. Further back, behind the main house, was the carriage house which was an impressive feature in itself. Two-story, red brick with a high, peaked loft that raised the roof line of the "small house" to over forty feet in height.

Behind the house stretched acres of open field that sloped downward to a woodland with a creek running through it, filled with waterfalls and pools.

Robin's friend had an aunt on the east coast that had seen the real estate listing and had recognized the name of the town. The aunt had sent it to Robin's friend and had asked her if she knew there was a house like this in her town.

She did indeed know. After yoga classes, she and Robin would often drive out of their way just to pass by the large, old Victorian and look at it, and wonder what it must be like inside, and what kind of people lived in a place like that. Robin loved the Broadway house the same way that Mary, in "It's A Wonderful Life" loved the old Granville House. It was grand, but it was more than that. It had presence. It spoke to you. And as it would turn out, Robin was not the only one to have heard that voice.

Robin pulled the listing up on her laptop and starting looking through the pictures that were on the listing. She had never seen the interior before and was discussing each picture over text with her friend when I walked up. She turned her screen around and pointed at the listing and said, "Please buy this for me."

So, I did.

Well, at least that is how it would have gone if this were a movie and if we were wealthy. The actual mechanics of how we went from a nice home in a modern and easily reproducible development, to a completely impractical and uniquely frustrating non-modern home was more Rube-Goldberg in its incorporation. The first thing that I did was to call the bank to see if it was even possible. This was not one of those casual, "let me call my bank" moments, where "the bank", embodied in the gruff but jovial voice of a man who smokes cigars on his yacht, laughingly assures you that there should be no problem with "moving around a few things" to free up the money for it. This was a three-day long process of contacting several banks and mortgage brokers whose response was usually along the lines of either an incredulous "You want to do what?!?", or occasionally an uncomfortable silence as they contemplated the most polite way to respond to my absolutely ludicrous request.

After three days though, I found a broker who was actually enthusiastic about the project, and he went to work. After supplying them with copious documents, from tax records to income statements to letters of reference from my fourth grade English teacher, we finally put a package together that would get us pretty close to where we needed to be. First hurdle achieved.

The next step was to schedule a walk-through of the home. I didn't want to scrape together just enough money to buy the home and then have nothing left over to fix it up the way it deserved to be. It was entertaining to watch the scenes in "It's A Wonderful Life" where Jimmy Stewart and Donna Reed stick newspapers over the window to keep out the rain, but that was not the way I wanted to live.

There were a lot of issues when I did the walk-through, but none of them seemed to be showstoppers. Technically, the house was move in ready, and we could have chosen to just move in and do nothing to it, but our goal was restoration, so there was a lot that needed to be done to make it not only livable but to bring it back up to a standard that would allow it to host events and be a part of the community again as it was always intended to be.

I did all of this without telling Robin. I wasn't going to bring up the discussion of actually buying it unless I knew there was at least some outside chance that we could pull it off. Once I had everything lined up, I scheduled another walk-through and asked Robin if she wanted to go and take a look at it.

Initially, she said no. She thought I had called the realtor and posed as an interested buyer just so that she could see firsthand what it looked like inside. She longed to see the inside, but she didn't want to be rude, and thought it would be disrespectful to waste the realtors time. When I told her that I was serious and had already set up potential financing and had done an initial walk-through to make sure there weren't any major problems, she was gob smacked. She was certain that I couldn't be serious. I think she probably felt that way through the entire process.

And it was a lengthy process. We made our first offer but then before we even had a chance to think about it, we were informed that a couple from out of state had made an all-cash offer for over the asking price and that their offer had been accepted. So just like that, as quickly as it had begun, it seemed like the story was over.

We spent the next two weeks playing the "what if" game and sighing about the house, while at the same time congratulating ourselves for avoiding what would have been a decision that placed emotion far ahead of financial responsibility. Then we got a call from the realtor informing us that, after further discussion and inspection, the first couple had backed out of the deal. We were back in the game.

It should have been a clue for us that the first couple backed out. It probably was, but like most emotional decisions we tend to ignore clues that don't line up with what we have already decided is the best outcome for us.

There were still other interested parties though. We were not the only ones. For the next several weeks, we went through a daily stream of calls and text messages where we would tell the realtor our final offer and then a counter-offer would be made or someone else would make a better offer, and we would come up with a new, final-final offer. Lather, rinse, repeat. For two weeks. I think we eventually got up to our final-final-absolutely-no-way-we-can-go-higher-we're-really-serious-this-time-final offer. We felt like we were getting close but there was still another interested buyer that we couldn't seem to shake, and the current owners were in no hurry to sell.

I was almost to the point where I was going to start looking through the couch cushions for loose change, or possibly asking one of the cats to get a job in order to find a few more dollars to increase our bid, when it occurred to me that I had something that it was unlikely the other buyer had.

Royalties.

Now to be clear, I am a barely-published author and the royalties from my children's books are enough to pay our coffee bill for the year, but they are not enough to purchase a home. It wasn't the children's books that I was thinking of though. I have other novels that I have written or that I am currently working on that I haven't shopped out to a publisher yet, so there was potential there. What if I offered the owner a percentage of the royalties from a book that had not been published yet?

It was madness. So crazy that I didn't even tell Robin about it when I wrote up the proposal and took it to the realtor. I could tell that the realtor had questions about my sanity too when I met her at the house the next day and handed her the offer. She said that she had never seen anything like this before, but that she would let the owners know and see what they said. She was very honest with her response to me and let me know that this was not something that was likely to work.

But the current owners didn't laugh, and they didn't reject it. They came back with a counter-offer. Not for more money, but for a greater percentage of the royalties. (The offer, by the way, was for a fantasy book that I wrote, called "The Tireless Ones." It is still unpublished.)

I was honestly a little shocked myself. I made a minor adjustment to their counter-offer and sent it back, and then I went back and told Robin. She was as amazed as I was and we stood there staring at each other, asking over and over again, "Does this mean what I think it means?"

For two days we waited to find out if it did in fact mean what we thought it did. If it meant that they were actually going to accept our offer. Then on the third day we got the call. They had accepted the offer. The contract was signed.

That ordeal though was only the second hurdle. The entire deal was contingent on our previous home appraising for a specific amount (it did not), a new inspection to be completed that showed there was no more knob and tube wiring in the house (there was), and a certification that the steps were in compliance with safety and accessibility requirements (they were not), to name only a few.

Even after the deal was accepted, there were about a dozen more reasons why the deal should have fallen through, but at every step, for some reason, it didn't. Even at the final walkthrough, on the morning of the closing, we heard some strange noises in the ceiling. Robin and I, and the realtor, and the owner all looked up and then looked at each other.

"Oh yeah. There might be raccoons in the attic," the owner said awkwardly, and then handed us the keys.

There would be an entire race track full of hurdles, but the book isn't about The Manor. It's about No Tail. I only tell you this much about the story because The Manor would quickly become such an important part of No Tail's story. Without The Manor, this book would likely not have ever happened.

11

I think The Manor was the last piece of the puzzle for No Tail's transition. Or perhaps No Tail was the last piece of the puzzle for The Manor. It's hard to know what the rules are when magic is involved.

I wrote a very boring paper once on long-term potentiation in neurons. The gist of it was that a neuron will either fire when it receives a single large electrical charge, or when it receives a series of small electrical charges in a short period of time.

Think of it like your bathroom sink.

Your bathroom sink will hold a certain amount of water. If it exceeds that amount, it will overflow. There is a drain in the sink so that in most cases, the water drains out of the sink faster than it pours in. If you dumped in a big enough bucket of water at one time though, it wouldn't have time to drain out and it would overflow. Or if you turned on both taps at full speed, you might get more water pouring in then will drain out so that eventually the water will fill the sink and overflow.

I think magic is like that. I think we all have a bit of magic about us, but it doesn't always activate. The charge isn't quite strong enough for it to become apparent.

I think places can accumulate a little of that magical charge as well. A kind of Leyden jar of wonder. For one hundred and forty years, The Manor had been storing up its charge.

If magic exists, then The Manor certainly looks like the place where it would happen. It is a red brick structure, situated just far enough off the main road to appear thoughtful without being aloof. It contains over nine thousand square feet in the main house, spread across three floors, with a full basement below, and a fourth floor attic above that leads up to a captain's walk, sixty feet above the ground below. It impresses without communicating pretension. It is grand, but approachable.

There is a two-story, three thousand square foot carriage house behind the main building, and the ruins of an old springhouse even further back behind that. The grounds extend down the hill from the buildings, across a field, into the woods and encompass a stream, complete with waterfalls. There are deer, foxes, coyotes, groundhogs, and all manner of wildlife that call The Manor home.

Inside the home, there is a library with rolling ladders, a ballroom, grand stairs, colored light filtering in from multiple stained glass windows, and even a sealed off room hidden in the basement. It is a place where raccoons play with silver coins in the attic.

We have found three separate stashes of hidden coins since we moved in, as well as books tucked into a secret reading nook, and items placed out of sight on shelves so high, they were forgotten for decades. If there are doors to other worlds, The Manor is where you would find them.

The story of The Manor includes pirates, the founding of the Rhode Island colony, and the women's suffrage movement. It has been accumulating those static charges of wonder for a hundred and forty years, and maybe even longer.

Then No Tail came along, and that was the final spark that was needed.

Almost immediately after we moved into The Manor, we started a social media page to keep people updated on our restoration projects. Mostly it was for friends and family. Everyone wanted to know what was going on with the big mansion that we had just bought, so instead of sending out a dozen different emails or responding to fifty different text messages, we decided it would be easier to just post the updates for everyone to see.

Within a week, we realized there were over three hundred people on our page. That was far more than our small circle of friends and family. As each week went by, more and more people came to the page. The magic spread.

As we passed five thousand, and then ten thousand people following the page, people began to send us letters and messages. Some of them were simply letters of thanks for sharing our journey, but some of them were incredibly personal stories that they felt compelled to share with us. They also began to send us packages that held items that they wanted us to have. Most of these were accompanied by notes that all communicated basically the same thing.

"I'm not sure why, but I felt compelled to send this to you."

"This felt like something that belonged at The Manor."

We received items with connections to the last queen of Hawaii, to Luke May, America's "Sherlock Holmes", to H.P. Lovecraft, and many more. What was even more amazing than the items themselves though, was how each one seemed to have a connection to something at The Manor that the sender could have never known about. Perhaps the most amazing thing we have received so far is a reproduction of a painting from a nineteenth century Polish painter that the owner "felt like we might like."

What the gifter could not have known was that a copy of that painting had been one of only two pieces of art that had hung in my house when I was a kid. It had belonged to my father. He of the hidden newspaper clipping who first introduced me to the idea of dying on a hill. I loved the painting when I was a kid. The wolf in the painting always reminded me of my father, and I had told my father that I would like to have it someday. Unfortunately, the painting was lost when my parent's house burned down many years ago.

But thirty years later, here it was.

Because someone "felt like it belonged here."

Every person has some spark of magic inside them, and as more and more people began to find The Manor, they added their own spark to the magic that No Tail and The Manor had started.

I know it sounds ridiculous, but somewhere inside the ridiculousness is a truth that calls out to people, reminding them of a dream that they hadn't thought of since they were little.

We all have these little sparks of the impossible that we see out of the corner of our eyes. Flashes of the divine that stand out against the drabness of the mundane. But they are gone so quickly that we would rather convince ourselves that they don't exist than risk following the will-o-the-wisp "what ifs" that lead us away from reason and into the unknown.

I have seen a hole in the center of my laptop and a corresponding hole in the back of my folding, metal chair, made by a piece of shrapnel that passed right through where my chest would have been if I had not gotten up only seconds earlier.

I have listened to an EOD tech explain to me that the detonation system in the two thousand pound IED that had been under my vehicle should have gone off.

I have stopped to speak to a priest that suddenly appeared at a tourist site in California and because of that conversation missed getting onto a bus that was the site of a fatal stabbing only moments later.

I was part of a plans team that created a reproduction of the "Band of Brothers" poster the week before a deployment, with our pictures photoshopped onto it in place of the actors. I was otherwise occupied though when they took the pictures so I was the only one whose picture was not on the poster. A year later, at the end of the deployment, I was the only one out of that group that was still alive.

All of these things, and a hundred more just like them, are just coincidences. Mere accidents. They happen all of the time. That is what we tell ourselves.

Religious people might call it divine intervention, but I hope that is not the case. I don't think that I would have much respect for a god that saw fit to save me but not Abbas. That doesn't sound like a divinity with compassion. That sounds like something that a god who sets up a folding table on the street would do, trying to lure the rubes into a game of three card monte.

"Follow the queen. Find the little lady, and I'll let you live. Over and under, under and over. Which card is it? Pick one."

Because those games are always rigged, aren't they? Only a fool would place his money down on the table and make that bet, and I don't want to believe that the cosmos is nothing more than a huckster with greased hair and a fake smile. I have no time for a busker god that performs for a disinterested crowd.

But there is something. My rationalist friends might call it a probability function played out across big numbers, but there is more kindness in it than that. My religious friends might call them god-winks, but there is more humility in it than that. Somewhere between omnipotence and absence, between quantum and canon, is where I reside. Considered a heretic by one side and a fool by the other.

I think Freddie would have understood. It's a kind of magic.

I think that's probably the best way to describe how No Tail, and The Manor, and I finally wound up together.

III

So five days before Christmas, in 2021, we all moved into The Manor. Robin and I, and No Tail, and Luna, and Thor, and Grayby, and Otis.

Have I not mentioned Otis and Grayby yet?

We have a lot of cats, y'all. I think the appropriate expression is "there's hella cats in here." So, forgive me if I forget to update them properly. Let me catch you up, because it is important. As dark as those twelve months were, when we lost three of our furry children in rapid succession, it is important to let you know about the moments of light as well.

Otis is a force to be reckoned with. We are fairly certain he is a force for good, but he has just enough crazy in him to keep his options open in case he decides to be a supervillain. He was a few months old in late 2020 when he walked out into the middle of the street and flopped on his side, directly in front of an oncoming SUV.

Fortunately for him, Robin was the one driving the SUV, or else his story might have ended rather abruptly. She stopped and opened the door, planning to get out and rescue him, but Otis, being the precocious cat that he is, saved her the trouble by leaping into the car, and perching expectantly, ready for whatever adventures lay ahead. In hindsight, Robin says that she's not completely sure that Otis might not have been trying to carjack her. Robin claimed at the time that she intended to put Otis into the foster system, but after getting to know him, she didn't trust anyone else to make sure that he didn't eventually build his own particle accelerator in the basement, so for the greater good of humanity, we kept him.

Grayby has a history going back several years with us. As early as 2016 we had seen a grey cat in our neighborhood that Robin began to call Earl Grey. Earl Grey would occasionally come onto the porch, but he was one of the most skittish cats we had ever seen, and we were never able to get close to him. Then one day we realized that it had been months since we had seen Earl Grey. He was never a frequent visitor so we don't know exactly when he disappeared, but it would eventually be another year before we saw another grey cat in our yard.

We started calling the new arrival "Grayby" but after looking at old photos and comparing the images, we figured out that Grayby was actually Earl Grey. By that time though, the new name had already stuck so he remained Grayby.

In the spring of 2021, not long after Salem had passed away, Grayby appeared on our back porch with one of his front paws barely hanging on. It was swollen and mangled, and from our vantage point it looked like it was opened up all the way to the bone. We immediately went into rescue mode and in short order, we had him at our vet who patched him up, saved his leg, and returned him to our rehabilitative care.

Grayby was an interesting case initially. He had no desire to be around people. People scared him. Of course, everything scared Grayby. He was one of the most timid cats I have ever met. There was next to no chance that he would show well at an adoption event, and we did not have the capacity to take on another cat, so it was our intention for Grayby to be another TNR. Except he refused to be R'd.

Our rehab room in the old house was a bedroom in the basement that had direct access to the backyard, but when we opened the door to let him return to from whence he came, he looked up and said, "No, thank you."

We explained to him that if he wasn't going to leave then he would have to integrate into the rest of the household. He said, "No, thank you" to that suggestion as well.

So those were the five personalities that we had to deal with as we sat there the first evening, staring at the piles of boxes, four years of accumulated dust, listening to the raccoons playing in the attic above us, wondering what in the world we had gotten ourselves into.

For the first few days, all of the cats were kept contained in two rooms. Part of this was a safety concern. With people and boxes moving in and out of the doors practically non-stop, we didn't want any cat escaping. Although no one was a particular flight risk, moving is stressful, and there is no telling what a stressed cat might do. Losing a cat under such circumstances would have tainted the already terrifying joy that we were feeling, now that owning The Manor had become a reality.

Additionally, if you are familiar with cats, you know that they are great at hiding. You can find yourself searching for a cat for an hour in an eight hundred square foot apartment. We were still unfamiliar with all of the nooks and crannies of the home, and the idea that one of our cats could wander for days through the nine thousand square feet, spread across four floors without being seen was a very real concern. In a house this size, they did not need to get outside to become lost.

For the time being then, it was good for them to become adjusted to a smaller space first, before we introduced them to the wider world that would soon unfold around them. It is impossible to imagine how we could have accomplished this with the old, murderous version of No Tail. We could have simply put him in his own room, as we had in the very beginning, but with the tumult of the move it would have been next to impossible to give him the proper amount of personal time.

Once the bulk of the move had been completed, we finally opened the doors and let the cats explore. The house had boxes everywhere, filled with familiar smells for them, but most of these things were still packed away, and the boxes were scattered all around unfamiliar rooms that were new and huge and strange.

Phryne, who was usually filled with nervous energy under normal circumstances, developed a new quirk where she would refuse to go up or down the stairs unless she was riding on someone's shoulders. Grayby immediately identified one of the rooms as his own and announced that the rest of the cats could wander through bizarro land if they wanted to, but he would stay right here, thank you very much. Thor reacted by racing relentlessly from room to room like the perpetual kid he was, exploring every corner and stairwell. Otis started cackling as he tried to decide whether to set up his secret lab in the creepy attic or in the creepy basement. Luna was mostly non-plussed, but she was not too pleased with all of the stairs.

No Tail was the least impacted of anyone. He didn't really have a reaction at all, positive or negative. He sauntered around his new palace, acknowledging the change but unconcerned by it all. He had already undergone the greatest shift in living conditions out of all of the cats, going from the environmental extremes of eastern Afghanistan to indoor living in the central United States.

Going from a comfortable home in Kansas to another home that only differed in size and scent would have been a non-event for a seasoned traveler like him.

Or perhaps he was comfortable with it because what had become important to him was his people, and as long as his people were there, he didn't care where "there" was.

There was one other very important shift in his personality that occurred shortly after we moved into The Manor. No Tail had already become comfortable enough in his sense of security that he would sleep around the other cats, and would engage in play with them, but he still had maintained that instinctual need to make sure his back was never exposed. Even on those occasions when he seemed to be asleep, if another cat or a stranger came into a room and walked behind him, he would shift his position, often without even opening his eyes, so that his back was repositioned and there was no one behind him.

He also had become accustomed to being petted, and would let you sit all day if you wanted to and stroke his head, but only his head. If your hand ventured back behind his line of vision, he would leap away, or possibly even bite you.

Once we moved into the new house though, it was not long before he simply relaxed wherever he happened to be. The need to constantly face an open doorway, even in repose, simply faded away without any precipitating event other than the move. He also stopped reacting if you petted him beyond his head.

There is peace in watching a cat relax. They can be twitchy animals, even under the best of circumstances, so when you see a cat flop down and really rest it is meditation in fur form. If you have never experienced it, it is hard to describe.

It is like the way that you can see the muscles in a tiger at rest and simply feel the powerful potential that they hold, whether they are moving or not. The power that is projected when those muscles relax is just as moving and confounding, but it is the power of release. A tiny nuclear reaction of calmness. And when those waves of calm pass through you, no matter how stressed or anxious you were feeling, for a moment you can share in the cat's sense of release of all concerns. It is always beautiful to watch a cat relax. Seeing No Tail let his last reservations and concerns go was like a Stendhal moment of beauty that transported you to some place where beauty was all there was. For that alone, the entire ordeal of buying the house was worth it.

The rest of his personality remained all No Tail, however. I have rarely met a cat as food motivated as he was. It is expected that a stray cat is always going to have some degree of food insecurity. When you add in the fact that, due to his stomach condition, No Tail had to be placed on a special diet that even the veterinarian described as "very bland", his pursuit of all things edible was extreme.

To complicate matters, he was magician-level quick. He might sit on the counter two feet away from your plate, and you could carefully run through the calculations of how long his arms were and what the friction coefficient of the counter is and what the speed of light in a restored Victorian kitchen is when acted upon by a black cat, and you might come to the conclusion that there is no physical way that he could get to your plate and grab your burger before you could react in time to stop him from getting it, and you would be wrong.

I recall one time in particular that I was literally extending my fork to pick up a piece of sausage, and suddenly it wasn't there. No Tail, who had been standing on the floor next to the table, easily four feet away, had somehow levitated up to the table and nabbed the sausage from my plate in the time it took my hand to move about three inches. He was now happily sitting on the table, still several feet away, chewing away on his purloined snack. I tried explaining to him that it wasn't even real pork, and it was just soy and mycoprotein, but he either did not care, or he was fully supportive of my vegetarian choices.

It was pointless to try and get it back from him. Once he acquired a piece of taboo food, it was his. On those rare occasions that you forgot that he was a cat and that you were a human and tried to retrieve the stolen morsel, he would switch into Hollywood car chase mode, and the soundtrack would kick in as he careened off of furniture and over obstacles, staying just out of reach of the pursuing person.

Moving to The Manor only made it worse. There were multiple sets of stairs and a seemingly endless string of rooms to run through, so there was no way that you were going to corner a cat like him. The best you could do when he managed one of his culinary heists was to ask him politely to consume it in the kitchen so you wouldn't have to clean cheesy grease residue off of a piece of antique furniture.

No Tail might give up the rage and the anxiety, but he would never give up his tuna.

IV

Much of what drew people to our page initially was the obvious attraction of the house itself, but a part of the magic was the addition of the cats. The cats soon developed a following of their own, and people began to respond to them and even message them occasionally. We began to post more about the cats and allow each of them to develop their own personality.

Thor and Otis quickly became crowd favorites. Thor took his natural fearless and inquisitive nature to new levels at The Manor. While doing renovations that involved converting an old linen closet into a laundry room, we had to cut into the wall to gain access to the plumbing and electrical systems. Thor took this as an opportunity to explore.

The walls and the floors at The Manor have spaces between them that are exceedingly wide. Straight out of a classic Gothic novel. I have crawled into them myself a few times, so it was nothing for a small orange cat to dash into a hole in the wall and disappear. He could have wandered for days between the floors and within the walls, and after an hour of trying to get him out, we were beginning to have visions of the fire department cutting holes through the hand-carved wood paneling to rescue him. Fortunately, 9-1-1 was not needed and he came out on his own, covered in hundred year old soot and dust.

In addition to his Indiana Jones adventuring, he also had a sunny disposition that many orange cats have, and he became an encouraging voice that constantly reminded everyone about the positive things about themselves.

Otis began to showcase his version of a mad genius that was tucked inside the most adorable stuffed animal. He might offer his opinion on quantum entanglement one day, and then delve into the question of which dinosaur would make the best butler the following day. With Otis, people were never quite certain that he might not take over the world one day, but he was so lovable that they wouldn't really care if he did.

Luna became the jazz diva and historian, and Phryne began to gain popularity as the author of her own advice column.

People generally seemed to enjoy all of their unique personalities but would often gravitate toward one or the other as a particular favorite. Regardless of which cat was someone's professed favorite, or whether someone was following our story because of an interest in old home renovation, No Tail seemed to find universal appeal across all interests and all demographics. People were drawn to his story, and from the very beginning, they began to ask for a book that would tell them more.

Three years later, that request has finally become the reality that you are holding in your hands today.

V

None of this exposure or interaction was expected, and there were more than a few times when Robin was feeling a little overwhelmed and was tempted to just shut the whole thing down. Gradually though, we began to adjust to it and even to embrace the opportunities that it provided. We decided to use the reach of social media to provide more awareness for the rescue groups that we supported, and to begin to build a broader network of rescuers across the country. Inevitably though, it also began to generate problems for us as people began to message us almost daily with requests to rescue a particular cat or to pay for operations for a cat in need, or in many cases, to bring a new cat into our home to live at The Manor.

This became a struggle for me. Although there is often a trope that is presented wherein the woman is the one bringing home stray cats and the man is the one that has to say no, in our case the roles were reversed. Robin has had to frown at me, more than once mind you, when she has found me outside talking to one of our resident coyotes, and one of our newfound internet friends even sent me a stuffed skunk on one occasion when I mentioned in a post that Robin wouldn't let me pet the baby skunks that came up to me in the garden. There was even a resigned shake of her head recently when we trapped a squirrel in the attic and I informed her that I had let it go back into the attic because it was raining outside.

It wasn't that Robin didn't want to rescue animals as well. We would never have been a good fit if being a rescuer was not also part of her DNA. It was just that she tended to be the more reasonable one and point out the obvious things that alluded me, such as, you can't keep wild raccoons as pets, or injured deer cannot be rehabilitated inside the house, or, no, for the love of Pete, you cannot turn the basement into an aviary!

Not only did she have to struggle with my attention span that was never anywhere near as grand as my plans, but she also had to deal with the way that PTSD impacted my need to rescue. Which was even more problematic for her, since she had her own trauma-generated need to rescue. Basically, I was asking her to be the adult in the room while I played Doctor Dolittle.

So the constant messages imploring us to save this cat or this dog began to generate a new stressor that we were unprepared for. We started serving as a temporary foster on occasion, and as a go-between for people in need and people with the means to help. In 2023, our resolve collapsed under the pressure.

I first saw the message about Simon while we were having breakfast one morning, and I knew immediately that he would be coming to live with us. So certain was I that I even considered deleting the pictures before Robin saw them because I knew the moment she laid eyes on him, we would be bringing him home to "foster" and that he would never leave.

No Tail was sitting in his usual place at breakfast. Within easy paw reach of my plate in case I got distracted. I was distracted by the message on my phone but I had already finished my breakfast so there was no risk of food thievery. I looked over at him to see if he could provide me any logical reason not to show the picture to Robin. We were in over our heads with time commitments and financial commitments. We couldn't afford to take on another cat, especially one that we already knew would have extensive vet bills. And when would we have the time for it?

No Tail just looked at me and said, we'll figure it out.

Shaking my head in resignation, I showed Robin the pictures.

Simon had been part of a hoarding situation, and when the woman caring for him had lost her trailer house, all of the cats were turned out. Some wound up at shelters, but many wound up as strays. Simon was one of them.

Simon desperately did not want to be a stray. He was reported to have been going up to different doors in the trailer park and asking to be let inside, but no one there had the ability to care for him. He wound up spending that winter outside and was unprepared for the exposed life he was suddenly thrust into.

Temperatures that season were below zero for extended periods of time. Simon developed frost bite on his feet and on his ears. The frost bite on his ears became infected. Had he not at last been taken in to a local rescue by a kind soul, he would not have made it to summer.

He wound up losing both of his ears, and he had to have surgery on his head to clean out the infection. When we first saw him, the top of his head had been shaved. It looked like a tonsure and, combined with the expression on his face, it gave the overall impression of an angry, drunk monk.

A few months after Simon came to live with us, our digital exposure led another rescue to our door. An eviction gone wrong had allowed a mother cat and two kittens to escape. The residents had come back and gotten the mother cat, but their new residence would not allow them to keep the kittens. One was put into a local adoption center, and the other was trapped late one evening, when Robin and I were the only ones available to react.

Things were not going as swimmingly as we had hoped at that point in our manor adventure. We had been in the new home a year and a half and had already gone through the entire budget that we had planned to last us for five years, and then some. We had recently added to our cat total, and that addition had been a high health risk which meant that it had also been a high financial investment. We had had a contractor steal over ten thousand dollars from us, the taxes on the house had doubled, and every day we seemed to find a new thing that needed to be fixed. And to top it off, my car had just died. The thought of bringing in a new cat and taking on another expense, even a small one, seemed overwhelming to me.

Fortunately though, Robin assured me that we were at no risk of keeping this cat. A friend of hers had already seen the pictures and wanted the cat for herself. All we had to do was pick the cat up, take care of it a few days, and then it would go on to its new home.

I was so confident that he was not staying that I even made a post on line, showing everyone our latest rescue, but loudly declaring that he was not staying. I should have known better. The universe doesn't like being challenged like that. Robin's friends situation changed and suddenly Max had nowhere to go.

Max had a big attitude for such a little kitten, and he was already exhibiting annoying little brother habits with the other cats, even No Tail.

"We can't keep him," I told No Tail. "I have no idea what we are going to do."

No Tail looked at me and repeated, we'll figure it out.

So, Max stayed, and with each new addition, there was an adjustment period with all of the cats except No Tail. He had gone from an isolated, raging cat that wanted to kill anyone that invaded his home or threatened his resources, to the one that had to reassure me that if there were people or animals that needed our help, it was our obligation to help them. No Tail demonstrated that he had not only embraced the idea of peace, which can be a solo pursuit, but that he had also learned empathy and compassion, which requires action.

VI

Although Max demonstrated some snarky, and even occasionally spoiled kid, behavior, he integrated quickly into the rest of the group. Simon, however, was dealing with some trauma of his own and that had created conflicted behaviors which made his integration more drawn out. He had a desire to be with people, but his default stress reaction was violence. We kept him in his own bedroom suite initially to give him time to heal from his surgeries, and to decompress, and would set aside time to sit with him every day to socialize him.

He loved being petted and would gladly sit there all day and snuggle with you. The problem was that he would get happy and excited when you petted him, and when he was stimulated, he would bite. That was the only reaction he knew. Then if you drew away from him, it became even worse. He was so paranoid that he would be abandoned again that he would actually run to the door and try and block you from getting out. If you tried to go around him, he would attack you.

It is obviously counterproductive from an outside view. He wanted to be loved, and if you stopped loving him, he would threaten to attack you unless you came back and loved him again. If we had been dating, our friends would have told us we were in a toxic relationship.

It got so bad that Robin could not go into the room without support. He would attack her even more violently if she tried to leave. At first, she thought that he hated her, and would likely wind up being a cat that bonded mostly to me, but it was actually the opposite. His desire to be with her was so strong that in his stimulated state he lost his little kitty mind.

This reaction continued even after his initial integration and was so strong that he would attack other cats when they would get near Robin. Fortunately, not too long after he began his new life, he made the mistake of attacking No Tail.

Robin was going downstairs, and Simon was following her as he always did, when Robin called out to No Tail. Simon knew the other cats by name already, and as soon as his mom spoke to another cat, he spun around to see where No Tail was, and launched himself at him.

Simon weighs about twelve pounds, and No Tail was down to about seven at the time. Simon was two years old, and No Tail was fifteen. Had it come to a fight, all of my money would have been on No Tail. Simon barreled into him, and knocked him over, and then No Tail did one of the most amazing things that I have ever seen.

He turned and looked at Simon, and Simon froze.

It was not one of those steely eyed, tough guy looks that lets you know that you have tangled with the wrong cat. There was no threat in it. No Tail's gaze did not warn Simon of past battles and of potential violence yet to come. It was a look that was weary of violence.

Something passed between the two of them in that moment. If No Tail had been a Jedi, he might have said, "This is not the fight you are looking for." Perhaps he told Simon that this is not the way things are done at The Manor. Perhaps he warned him what awaited people that chose the path of violence.

Whatever it was, Simon's demeanor changed from that day on. He is the largest cat in the house, yet no longer does he ever initiate violence, and he rarely even raises his paw in defense when another cat tries to initiate a fight. He will either ignore it completely, or walk away, or occasionally turn and look at us as if he is confused as to why someone would choose violence when there are better ways.

A friend of mine once asked me how I would like to die, if the choice were left to me. My response to her was that for me, an ideal death would come after a long life, but that in the end, when death was near, I would want the opportunity to raise myself one more time from my sick bed, pick up my sword, and die defending what is good. Hopefully on a hill, of course.

That old "blaze of glory" turnip.

I am confident that No Tail could have roused the tiger again when Simon attacked him, and he would have been glorious in his resurrected violence, but that was not how No Tail wanted to live the last of his days. When he put down his sword, he put it down for good and for all.

I didn't hear everything that passed between No Tail and Simon that day, but I got the gist of it. And No Tail was right. It was not long after this incident that I contacted my friend and said, "I want to change my answer." I told her that for me, the perfect death would not come with sword in hand but with a spade. The idea of dying in conflict. Dying with rage in my mind, justified or not, seems less appealing. I don't want my death to be what gives me meaning. I want my life to have meaning.

I have a garden that I love to tend. If I could choose my passing, many years from now I would love to spend a summer morning out in my garden, tending my flowers, and when my exertions had tired me out, I would like to lean back against one of the benches while the sun shines down on my face, and rest my eyes for a minute. I would like to drift off to sleep with the scent of flowers and the warmth of the sun around me.

And then I would love to awaken to the insistent howl of a black cat, telling me that it was time to get up and that I was late with his tuna.

Conveniently, the garden at The Manor is on a bit of a hill. It is not much of a hill, but it is enough.

VII

One chapter to go. We are getting close to the end, so it is time to tie up a few loose ends if we can. I have gotten several comments and questions over the last three years that refer to No Tail's philosophy, so this feels like an appropriate place to address it.

It feels odd to talk about the philosophy of a cat. He didn't wear a robe and give lectures in the forum, or wear tweed jackets and hold classes at Cambridge. He didn't stare for hours into a candle, or travel to a remote cave to commune with the universe. The first time that I saw someone refer to his "philosophy" though, it rang true, and I knew that I would have to at least try to address it, although I know that whatever I write down in these few pages will be inadequate.

Perhaps the best place to start would be with two of our favorite movies that we often enjoyed watching together. "The Princess Bride" and "It's a Wonderful Life."

"It's a Wonderful Life" was released in 1946. Jimmy Stewart and Donna Reed. Great movie. If you haven't seen it, go watch it. We'll wait.

Pretty good, wasn't it?

Did you know that the censors had strong misgivings about allowing the movie to be released? The bad guy in the film, Mr. Potter, is never brought to justice. George Bailey never marches into his office and punches him in the nose. The police don't discover that he stole the money from George and drag Potter away in chains. The bad guy just goes on being bad.

"The Princess Bride" was released forty years after "It's a Wonderful Life", and if you pay attention, there are a lot of similar themes presented in both movies. The bad guy not being punished is one of them.

Fred Savage's character asks his grandfather, "Who kills Humperdinck?", to which his grandfather replies, "No one." Fred Savage then responds with one of the most quoted lines from the film.

"Jesus, Grandpa! What did you read me this thing for?!"

Shouting out at the narrator and demanding to know what was the point of it all sounds a lot like life sometimes.

The point of the movies isn't that justice was served. The point of the movies is that goodness endures. If that is not something that you can live with then you probably won't like the movies. There's probably going to be a lot of life that you won't like either.

No Tail's philosophy would start with the premise that goodness must be the end that we seek, and that we must seek it for goodness' sake alone. We can't seek goodness with the belief that justice will be served or that good will win. If winning is our focus, then we will begin to side more with power than with goodness.

That final encounter, when Simon attacked him, No Tail was not seeking a fight. Simon was the aggressor. No Tail would have been justified in retaliating. But if his ultimate objective was peace, then he had to be willing to not mete out justice to Simon for his actions.

In a world that is so filled with injustice, this is a difficult lesson to learn. It is a hard philosophy to follow.

We are conditioned to want balance. There is always debate about how that balance is best achieved. Do we cut off the hands of the thieves? Do we take an eye for an eye? Do we strike back at the person who strikes us?

Unfortunately, our desire for balance can be easily corrupted, and there are many who would seek to convince us that revenge and balance are the same thing.

We want the bad guy to pay. We need it. Sometimes we need that part of the equation so badly that we invest all of our energy into seeking retribution and have nothing left to invest in seeking what is good.

The world is so full of stories of cruelty and injustice. How many times have you seen or read a story about someone doing something despicable and thought, "I hope that they get what's coming to them," or something even less kind? I assure you there is no judgment coming from me if you have. Working in animal rescue as we do, we have seen things that would make your blood run cold, and the things that I have wished upon the people responsible come straight from that monster that lives inside of me that grins any time blood flows.

I think No Tail's philosophy would involve seeing cruelty and injustice and thinking, "I hope that the person responsible has a change of heart and becomes a better person."

Leon Uris once wrote that the greatest human power is the power of redemption. I think that goes for cats as well.

Redemption over revenge.

Compassion over justice.

Goodness over power.

Those would be the cornerstones of any philosophy that No Tail might offer. These are all things that he tried to teach me in our time together. I was not the best pupil.

I would like to say that I reserve my outrage for only the worst offenses. For those times that children or animals are mistreated, and the innocent are abused. But I have spent a large part of this book itemizing all of the reasons that is not the case. I struggle to modulate my responses. My reaction to being cut off in traffic may be as vitriolic as my reaction to seeing those in power trample on the rights of those who have nothing.

Anger becomes its own reward. It promises immediate gratification.

Redemption takes time. It's like a tree. It needs care and patience. The reward comes years later. You would think that as a gardener I would get that. I'm designing a hedge maze that will take ten years to complete, and I'm okay with that, but when it comes to balance, I want it right now. When I have seen so much of the darkness and have been struck more times than I care to count, I don't want to fight for goodness. I just want to fight. I just want to clench my fists and shout, "It's not right."

There are times to fight. As much as I talk about letting go of anger, that does not mean that there are not legitimate moments where you have to stand up and draw a line. There are hills worth dying on. There are still causes worth fighting for physically as well as emotionally. Thoughtless pacifism is as dangerous as senseless violence. But if fighting becomes all we ever do, we wind up devaluing those things that are actually worth fighting for. We begin to lose the distinction between the absolute and the convenient.

If we are as quick to fight when someone uses inappropriate language as we are when someone strives to suppress language itself, we have effectively equated the two things. If we clench our fists when someone becomes aggressive to fans of an opposing sports team with as much resolve as we do when someone threatens the life of a child, then we have placed that child's life in the same category as athletic ego. And if we cannot recognize the distinction between the two then we have no right to raise our fists at all.

I believe that No Tail would have fought if necessary, but he discovered that those necessary moments of violence are far fewer than what we want to believe they are. Violence is convenient. It usually eliminates the need for discernment. No Tail chose discernment over convenience.

I was too caught up in pointing out the myriad examples of unfairness and violation of innocence and the mutation of order that I viewed everything as yet another blow, and lived in darkness, repeating the same phrase, over and over again, like a madman.

"It's not right. It's not right. It's not right!!!"

But No Tail suffered as many blows as I ever did, and spent as much time in the darkness, and in the end he chose to put aside violence and find another way. He would agree with me and tell me, yes, it's not right, but sometimes we have to be okay with that.

No Tail Says Goodbye

"What do you do though when you simply can't run anymore?" she asked.

Rodica drew in a deep breath and sighed. There was a tired smile on his face when he replied to her.

"You just keep running."

From, **"The Tireless Ones"**, by Thad Krasnesky

I

The old theater adage is "always leave them wanting more". You don't want people rushing for the exit after the last number is sung and the last lines are spoken. You want them glued to their seats, hoping that it's not over, even when they know that it is. Or better yet, you want them leaping to their feet, begging for an encore, shouting for one more moment of your time. No matter how good a performance is, if it goes on too long, there will be that inevitable moment where people start glancing at their watches or looking at the exits.

Every now and then though there is a performance that you truly want to never end. When the music is so good, and the performances are so perfect, and every note seems to resonate with your soul so that you are convinced that you could stay in that theater for the rest of your life and be perfectly happy if the show never ended. There is no amount of it that could ever make you not want more. You don't want the show to "leave you wanting more." You want the show to never leave. But in life, as well as in theater, there is always that moment when the curtain must go down.

No Tail always had two great drives in life; food and affection. That first morning when he chose to not eat breakfast, we knew. We pretended not to. No Tail had been with us for eight years at that point, and he had spent about half of that time almost dying, so we frowned our concerned frowns at each other and commented on how he must be having another one of his bad spells again. We would take him to his veterinarian, and they would run tests and we would give him some new medicine and try some new food and then in another two years from now we would all stand around again in amazement that he was still alive and talk about, "Remember two years ago when we were concerned that he was going to die again?"

But this time we knew.

In addition to his loss of interest in food, we had begun to see other signs. No Tail had an amazing physicality that we have mentioned before. His leaping ability was second to none. Powerful and sure-footed. When we moved into The Manor, before we began our renovations, there was a spot above the refrigerator that had a cabinet with a space above it, similar to his old cabinet hide-out in the previous house. One day, I found No Tail sitting on top of this space.

It was eight feet from the ground. There was no adjacent counter he could have leapt from. At that time, he was already fourteen years old. Most cat experts will tell you that eight feet is the absolute limit even for a young healthy cat, let alone a senior cat with serious health issues, yet there he was. Undeterred by age or illness.

But in 2023, shortly after Christmas and only a few weeks before he began to lose interest in his food, No Tail had come into the bedroom to help me get dressed as he did every morning. This usually consisted of him sitting on the bed while I alternated between buttoning up my shirt and petting him. He walked into the room as usual, walked up to the bed, and leapt.

And my invincible, champion leaper, slipped.

The bed is a tall bed, about three feet from the ground to the top of the mattress, but this was nothing for an athlete like No Tail, yet his leap carried him only about two feet up, where he had just enough reach to snag his front paws over the edge of the sheets. He scrabbled briefly for purchase before sliding ignominiously back to the floor. He looked up at me, as startled as he might have been if I had just grown three heads.

The confusion on his face at his failure to leap onto the bed was painful to see.

His steps became less sure after that day, and his reaction to his food told me the rest of what I did not want to hear.

We didn't talk about it that day. It was like we had reverted to superstitious medieval peasants who were convinced that saying the thing would somehow summon the thing. Don't say "bear" because it might cause a bear to appear. Instead, say "bee wolf." Talk around the thing. But never say the thing.

So that day we talked a lot about "bee wolves." We talked about adding supplements to his food to increase his appetite. We confidently observed that giving him some subcutaneous fluids would probably perk him right up. We remarked that he was looking a little tired.

But when the bear has already appeared, there is no point in calling it by a different name. Saying "bee wolf" won't make the bear disappear. When he licked at his food that evening but didn't finish it, we knew the bear was already there. We spoke no more of the bee wolves.

No Tail was much less hesitant to talk about his upcoming departure. Perhaps because he was an animal and was less conflicted about the natural order of things, or perhaps it was because he had achieved that level of peace that I was still seeking.

That night, as Robin and I lay in bed, with No Tail resting in his customary spot in the crook between my shoulder and my face, we talked about the preparations and the timing. I reasoned that the best choice would be to wait until the following Friday to bring him in. Since he wasn't in any immediate distress, that would give us plenty of time to make reasoned and well-planned preparations. We would schedule things so that we could focus on being with him, and not be distracted by what comes next. We would put a plan in place and the plan would free us up to fully enjoy our last few days together.

Even then, No Tail understood. He pressed his face against mine and told me that it was not the right decision, but that he understood why I was making it, and that it was okay. He assured me that it would all work out in the end and the important thing to remember was that he loved us, and that he was glad that we had brought him home.

11

For those of you that have never personally witnessed the process of someone becoming ill and passing away, it is shocking how quickly these things can progress. The rapidity of it often makes you want to deny that it is real. No one can go from simply feeling poorly to dying in twenty-four hours, so the fact that it happened so quickly is itself proof that they aren't really dying.

It's why death on a battlefield can often feel unreal. How can you turn around in the middle of a conversation and then turn back to that person a second later and they have a hole in their body and the body is still there, but the person is gone? Reality can't change that quickly so obviously what you are seeing can't be real.

No Tail and I had seen our share of battlefield deaths. Often enough that it should have lost its ability to shock us, but apparently it had not, because by the following morning I was still struggling to believe it. Neither Robin nor I had slept much that night. I think that there was likely not a moment throughout the entire night where at least one of us was not awake and gently stroking No Tail's head and face.

We had called all our family members the previous evening when we had made the decision to take him in at the end of the week and help him cross over, but that morning I realized how selfish that decision was. What I was secretly hoping for was that if we just waited a few more days, we would get one more miracle and he would shake it off as he had done in the past and then we could go back to life as usual, and the play would go on.

When I looked at my friend that morning though, I finally understood what he had been telling me. He would go on for the rest of the week if that is what I wanted. If that is what I needed. He would hang on even as his body started to shut down and force himself to keep going if it would help me deal with the loss, because although his great drive for food had faded, his other great drive, love, was still as strong as ever. He reassured me that he loved me enough to endure whatever was necessary to ease my pain.

There are so many lessons that he tried to teach me in our short time together that weren't always successful, but this was one that I had learned. It was the most painful, the most horrible, of all of them. Out of love, he would have endured for us as long as he could. So out of love, I chose to let him go.

We made all the calls again. Not because we wanted to cause anyone else to hurt, but because they deserved the respect of knowing. Several people offered to be with us or help out in any way if we needed it, but in the end, I knew that my grief would fill up too large of a space to allow other people around me so later that morning, Robin, Isabelle, and I got in the car with No Tail and headed to Blue Springs.

The details of the event itself are not important. We could morbidly describe the physical, step-by-step process but the only important thing to communicate about it is that it was done with the utmost respect and reverence, and that when he did pass away, we were holding him, and petting him, and telling him how much we loved him.

III

As a soldier, I have attended more memorial services than I can count or care to remember. As someone who has always been associated with animal rescue in one way or another, I have been present at the passing of far too many animals. I have been intimate with death.

My experiences have crossed many cultural and religious boundaries, so I have seen the way that death is handled by different people in different places from vastly different belief systems. My occupation has made me not simply an observer of these practices but has required that I study them in order to better understand the beliefs behind them.

The question of what happens to us after we die is fairly universal. It is one of the more common points of discussion at funerals whether you are Christian or Muslim, Jewish or atheist, humanist or Wiccan. Because of my background and experience, it is not an uncommon question for people to bring up to me whether a funeral is pending or not.

Every belief system has their party line. In animal rescue it is common for us to talk about animals crossing the rainbow bridge. And since we are nearing the end of the book, I suppose that this would be the time where people would ask me, "What happens next?" "Do you think you will see No Tail again?"

On a conceptual level, the question of whether or not I will see No Tail again is the wrong question to ask. It implies that I don't see him still. I did not learn everything that he had to teach me. Not for lack of trying. He had a difficult pupil to work with. But I did learn enough that I see him every time someone chooses justice over convenience and compassion over justice. I see him in those moments of peace that shine through the always present clouds of rage. Everywhere there is love, I see him.

Even in this book, which was the result of an accidental social media presence, he is there. How can someone ask if I will see him again when I see the impact he has already made in hundreds of lives? He will always be there because of the people to whom he mattered. I see him every day. Even in my own clumsy attempts to be better. To let go of my grief and my pain. In helping others to let go of their pain. He is always there.

But I know that's not what you are asking. You aren't asking for a concept or a figurative answer. You are asking for a definite yes or no answer. Do I believe that I will see him again? Is there an afterlife for pets? Is there an afterlife for us?

Well, let me give you a list of about a hundred books that address this topic, and then once you are done with those, we can read the next hundred, and then let's bring in the top hundred experts on the field to discuss it, and at that point we might be ready to begin to frame out what is true and what isn't. Some of these books will offer answers, but most will only lead to more questions. A few will try to offer reassurance. One of the most comforting references to the afterlife actually comes not from a book of faith but from a book of fiction by Stephen King. He refers to it in one of his books as "the clearing at the end of the path." I like that. That is more reassuring to me than any talk about clouds or angels or Elysian fields. An afterlife that is a clearing at the end of the path sounds like the kind of place that I would enjoy.

But enough discussion, right? You want a definitive answer. Not philosophical meanderings.

I will give you your definitive answer in the same way that I live my life. I believe by doing. As much as I would like to distill everything down to a mathematical formula and as much comfort as there is in that, most of my life has been one of action. I run into fires not because I have calculated the odds and have determined that I will not get burned, but simply because I believe that I will be okay. I charge into buildings not because I have analyzed the statistical probability of getting shot, but because I believe that I will be okay regardless of what the statistics say. I do not buy old houses because I know what I'm doing or because I've done the math and know that I can afford the necessary repairs and upkeep, but because I believe that passion will win out over numbers. I do not pick up an injured animal because studies show it will make me a better person or because I think I can perform miracles, but because I believe that I can help and because not rescuing them is not an option.

The truth is that I have been burned. I have been hurt. I have botched repairs and blown budgets. I have mourned those that I sought to rescue. But I have survived. And more often than not, action and belief have been a more effective approach than reason.

Belief is a difficult thing to hold onto at times. I'm not talking about irrational beliefs, like wearing the same socks makes your sports team win, or that aliens built the pyramids, or that fish is an acceptable topping on pizza. I'm not even talking about specific belief systems, like whether or not there is a heaven, or a god. This isn't a religious book any more than I am a religious person. It's just a book about a cat. But you can't spend time with a cat that has a soul that is as deep as No Tail's without believing that there has to be something. Sherlock Holmes tells us that once we have removed the impossible, whatever is left, no matter how improbable, must be the truth.

So, I will continue to run into fires, and rescue strays because I believe.

And somewhere, in a clearing at the end of the path, there is a black cat with a conspicuously loud voice and a conspicuously missing tail waiting for me. I will probably hear him long before I see him, but I will see him again.

Because I believe.

IV

There is a scene in Ted Lasso where Coach Beard is contemplating his relationship with Nate. Ted tells him that he hopes that "all of us, or none of us, are judged by what we do in our weakest moments, but instead by what we do with our lives if, and when, we are given a second chance." This statement ultimately guides Coach Beard's actions, and he goes on to tell Nate about how Ted gave him a second chance.

I think that No Tail gave me a second chance at life. I think that without him I would possibly be dead or in jail or homeless or who knows what. Maybe not. There's no way of knowing, and that's a lot of responsibility to put on a little cat, even retroactively, but I know that achieving anything that I have accomplished would have been immensely more difficult without him.

In Ted Lasso, Coach Beard tells Nate that what we do with our second chance is up to us. And so now it us up to me to decide what to do with the life that No Tail has given me.

I have friends that have struggled with all manner of addictions. I have counseled people with drug problems and am currently working with friends dealing with everything from relationship struggles to gambling addictions. I have often told people that, considering all that I have gone through, I am incredibly fortunate that I did not wind up addicted to anything. It would have been so easy to retreat into a bottle or pills or anything that would have soothed that trauma inside.

A common refrain is that the first step in solving a problem is to admit you have a problem in the first place. It is a step that until now I have never taken. I tell people that I have "anger issues" and feel like I am being pretty open about my struggles. I wrote about it earlier when I made my confession about seeking confrontations that were destined to end in violence. I have anger "issues." That is how I always frame it. It's an issue. I have issues.

It was only as I was writing this book that I realized it was not simply an issue. It was an addiction. As I helped other people try to frame their own addictions and find ways to reframe their lives in order to mitigate their addiction, I began to realize that the same phrases I was applying to other people's drinking or drug problems could be applied to my anger problem.

Too often people on the outside of addiction will look at the addict and try to help them by explaining to them how destructive their addiction is, but that approach rarely works. Do you think that someone who lives inside a bottle all of the time and destroys every relationship they are in doesn't realize that it is destructive? Do you think that the person who gambles away their rent payment every month and puts their family out on the street over and over again doesn't understand that that is a destructive behavior? Do you think that the person who has smoked for fifty years and is now breathing through a trach tube doesn't know that their addiction is destructive?

Addicts know. They're not stupid.

And I'm not going to get into all of the reasons for why someone might have an addiction problem. This isn't a psychology book. We can wander into an endless labyrinth of environment and genetic predisposition and chemical imbalance without ever actually facing the minotaur we came here to fight. But I do want to address at least one of the reasons that people remain addicts in spite of how absolutely damaging it can be.

And if you've gotten this far in the book, you know I jump around a lot, so let me make a quick illustrative side tour. Most people have things that they identify with. It gives them not only a sense of place and belonging, but it literally gives them their identity. It could be a sports team. It could be a hobby. It could be a religious movement, or a social cause, or their favorite sitcom. If we were able to analyze the way that someone spends their day and measure the intensity with which they engage in all of their past times, we could probably fairly accurately determine how they see themselves. We could put a metric to it. An identity statement might look something like, "I am an eleven percent husband, seven percent father, twenty three percent worker, thirty two percent softball player, twelve percent conservative, nine percent Atlanta Falcons fan, five percent religious person, and one percent Breaking Bad watcher."

If we were to take this person's favorite television show away, they wouldn't like it, but it wouldn't threaten their identity because ninety nine percent of them is still something else. Only one percent of them was identified with that television show. But if you took away their job or their ability to play softball, that would seriously strike at who they see themselves and would put their identity at risk. And even though that television show might not account for much as long as everything else stayed the same, what if someone broke their leg and could no longer play softball, which then led to them losing that relationship with the company softball team and eventually losing their job, which puts stress on their marriage and then they wind up getting divorced. Now you've suddenly taken away half of what that person sees themselves as. And if on top of that you then took away their favorite television show, that might be the piece that makes them feel like they are losing themselves. So they will cling to that so fiercely because the idea of losing who you are can be terrifying.

So, with that illustration in mind, much of an addicts identity is tied up in their addiction. You not only have to combat the mechanisms of the addiction, but you also have to fight that fear of losing who they are. Being an addict seems like a horrible thing to identify yourself as to those who aren't addicted, but when that is all you have, it is hard to give up.

Which brings me back to my anger issues.

My anger addiction.

It was not until I viewed my anger as something that I had to give up that I finally realized how big a part of me it had become. How much of my identity was tied up in just being angry. Admitting that it was an addiction, and accepting that it was something that needed to be given up was terrifying, because then who was I without it? Without my anger, what was left? What was the real me?

The exchange that I told you about earlier between No Tail and Simon had another important element to it, beyond its impact on Simon. It provided me a clearly defined opportunity to see No Tail, with his anger gone, but still one hundred percent himself. As I watched No Tail let go of his anger and rage and violence over the nine years we spent together, never once did I ever see him as anything less than himself. He wasn't losing parts of himself. When the anger was gone, No Tail remained.

The anger was never part of him.

It was only a circumstance. A disguise. A symptom. An impediment to becoming more. Because in that moment that he looked at Simon after Simon attacked him, No Tail was transcendent. There wasn't just a look on his face that rejected anger. There was a presence about him that embraced peace. A perfect peace that was ecstatically beautiful.

So perhaps I can lose my anger and not lose myself. I may never be as beautiful as No Tail was in that moment when he looked at Simon, but maybe the ugly parts inside me were never really me.

V

There are only a few pages left, so you might be starting to panic. There are too many loose ends that aren't tied up yet. And believe me, I am panicking right along with you.

Does our intrepid writer learn to put aside his anger?

Does he win the girl?

Do the raccoons ever move out of the attic?

I would love to say that I had my Thor moment. Where a singular incident occurred and from that glorious epiphany, I arose and raged no more. It would be a great ending, but it would be untrue. I am trying though. And I just wrote an entire book about it, so the pressure is on. It would be a huge waste of everyone's time if I blew up at someone cutting in line at the theater, and someone pointed at me and asked, "Isn't that the guy whose cat helped him control his anger?"

There is a reason that some religions have confession, and some treatment programs start with a statement of admission. It is a lot harder to step back from something once you have said it out loud. And I just said this to the entire world, or at least anyone who is willing to read this book. It would be an insult to any emotional investment you might have made in our story so far, and a betrayal of him if I didn't at least try.

Robin is still here. Just like struggling with my anger, there is no nice, concise conclusion to love either. Winning the princess is a lot easier than keeping her. The movie ends after they ride off into the sunset together, but after the credits are over and they are back at the castle, there are still going to be discussions about whose turn it is to clean the litter boxes or why someone can't remember to hang their swords up even though there are clearly hooks on the wall for hanging swords instead of just leaving them lying on the floor where someone can stub their toe on them and the vacuum cleaner can get tangled in the hilt.

Just last night, we had a moment of discussion where I was lost in my head for a few hours, having an internal discussion about all of the reasons that it was impractical and likely not possible to break into a Central American prison while simultaneously wondering if someone were to attempt it, what would be the best way to go about it, and I failed to notice that she had gotten her hair cut earlier that day. But for now, she is still here.

And the raccoons?

They have finally moved on.

Of course, I have said that before. I guess we'll see when fall rolls around.

When No Tail passed away in January of 2024, I was mentally healthier than I had been in a long time, but I was concerned about what might happen without him by my side. I am certain that anyone that knew me had those concerns as well. They were not unfounded. I had been unmoored when I had met him nine years earlier.

I think No Tail knew that The Manor was coming. I don't think that he knew the specifics, but even when he was consumed with anger, he had this odd connection to the world or the cosmos or whatever it is that might be out there. There was a depth and an understanding inside him that allowed him to tune in to things that other people don't see or hear.

When he let go of his anger, and hatred was no longer taking up bandwidth inside his head, I think that he was able to see even further. He could sense possibilities. I think that he felt that there was a thing out there that would give me the opportunity to pour my need to rescue into it, while maintaining its ability to rescue me in return, like he had.

So, with no evidence to support my belief, but with a certainty that is stronger than logic or reason, I believe that he waited for The Manor and I to meet. Maybe they even had conversations in whatever realm transcendent cats and sentient houses occupy. No Tail would have told The Manor how he had been broken when he and I had first met, but that gradually he had healed. He would have told her that I still had a long way to go to heal, miles to go before I slept, but that there was hope that I might get there some day if The Manor was patient.

I think he was pleased to leave me in The Manor's capable hands. She had already achieved that level of peace and compassion that No Tail had finally found. All she needed was some structural rescue and repair and she would be there not only for me, but for others as well, and for generations to come.

No Tail once told me, "You are not a large enough vessel to contain all of your sorrow. You must find something to pour your sorrow into or you will drown."

The Manor was something big enough for me to pour my rage into, and after his passing it was big enough for me to pour my sorrow into.

I believe that, for me at least, No Tail was a bodhisattva. A bodhisattva is an individual that achieves enlightenment and has the ability to ascend to whatever waits at the end of the cosmic escalator but chooses instead to stay behind to help others find peace as well. It was not something that came easy to him. He worked hard to get there. He gave of himself and eventually gave up himself to finally find rest. He did not get there by simply meditating. His battle was internal, but it was no less fierce than any physical battle that he ever fought. It was himself that he struggled with. There was not an outside force that he could conquer that would allow him to get where he wanted to be.

And it was clear to me that he did want to be at peace. He did not want to be angry anymore.

I want to want to not be angry anymore.

An acquaintance recently remarked that when they first met me, I seemed very polite and calm, and not the type of person that would ever fly off the handle. Then a situation arose that involved someone threatening one of the wild animals that live on the grounds of The Manor and he said it was like something passed over my face and I was gone. I had disappeared, and what was left behind looking back at him was not something pleasant.

I don't want to be gone anymore. I want to be present. I want to be here.

I don't think No Tail would have left if he didn't think I was ready. He was wiser than I will ever be, so I have to trust him on this one. I look forward to becoming the person that my cat believed I could be.

Three weeks after No Tail moved on, Robin got a message from the shelter about a young kitten who was likely going to be euthanized. This little creature had already lost one eye and was probably going to lose the other one as well. There was the possibility of additional injuries, and it was thought that even if he survived, it would be difficult to adopt out a blind cat, so the recommendation that had been made was that they just put the animal down. Without hesitating, Robin grabbed her keys. When I came home that evening, the triage bathroom had a new occupant.

Neither Robin nor I was ready for another cat. We were both still hurting from the loss of No Tail. But sometimes the one in need doesn't have time to wait for you to be ready.

That night, I spread out my sleeping bag on the floor of the bathroom and Nicholas Pyewacket, the newest resident of The Manor, curled up next to me in the sleeping bag and listened to me as I told him stories about the cat with no tail that had crossed continents and oceans to make sure that he would have a place to heal and find rest.

VI

And that is it. That is the Tale of No Tail.

Or at least part of it. No single book can ever contain the entirety of a person's life. Or a cat's.

There are also a lot of chunks of my story in there as well. Pieces of Robin's story. Bits of my kids stories are in there, and bits of stories from kids whose stories ended too soon. Various lengths of threads from the other cats that became woven into No Tail's fabric.

Pieces of you are in here too. If you are one of the ones that pushed for this book to be written, then this book is part of your story as well. If you are just reading this story, even if you weren't part of the initial push for it to be published, there are parts of you that are joined to us, and parts of us that are joined to you. You are part of No Tail's story, and he is part of yours. That is how magic works.

That is how life works.

It also means that I can blame you for any errors in the book. Any typos or grammatical errors, or places where I meandered off track and might not have successfully summed up what my point was and wound up on a completely different track. I wrote this book without an editor. No adult supervision. And we only have to look back to the great Ballroom Paint Fiasco of '25 to know what happens when I am unsupervised.

But at least the book got done. If I had waited until I had the time to finish it, or until I had a polished, edited product to send to a publisher, it likely never would have gotten done. You needed the book, and I needed to write it, and the end result is an imperfect, flawed product, which is as it should be, because the people in it are flawed. Me. You. All of us. We are all flawed.

Except perhaps for that one black cat with no tail. That one was perfect.

I have written and rewritten the ending of this book countless times already, which is unusual for me in many regards. I dislike fine-tuning things. I am a big-picture kind of person. The concept is usually enough for me and if the details are kind of fuzzy, well that's someone else's problem. Life is never still, so I tend to get things to the good enough point and then move on. There are probably parts of this book where you have already noticed that.

And there is still so much that has been left out. I have only just introduced you to Nicholas Pyewacket, and I haven't even mentioned Clawdius and Pantaloons, who joined us in the year since No Tail's passing.

Clawdius, my garden cat, who is content to just be with his dad while I write. The best writing partner I have had since our doofy panther, Salem passed away. Pantaloons, the Eliza Doolittle of our backyard who still has a lot of Covent Garden in her, but I am certain in time that she will become the duchess she was meant to be.

They all have entire stories of their own, from Thornton's "Adventures Within the Walls" to Simon's frost-bitten ears and tales of arctic survival. The Manor itself is probably a twenty-volume series, and we still have yet to discover nineteen of them.

And chapter after chapter that I could add about No Tail. Anecdotes and memories that could double the length of this book. The story itself is so easy to write.

The ending though…

I am fixating on the ending. I have written at least half a dozen endings so far, and have thrown away that many more, but it is time. I am going to have to stop writing soon.

I spent some time last night wondering why I couldn't just wrap it up with some quippy saying or philosophical observation and then move on. My initial thought was that it was a need to make it perfect. It was a tribute to No Tail, and I needed it to be perfect and complete, but there simply is no way. I could write for a hundred years, and I don't think that I could ever fully capture everything that I wanted to say.

That was part of it, I decided, but the greater reason was fear. I am afraid of the book ending because I am afraid that ending the book means that his story is over as well, and I can't think about that. I can't let his story end. So, I sit here and write, obsessively, overthinking what I said or what I didn't say because as long as my pen keeps moving or my fingers keep typing, I can keep his story alive, and I can keep him with me. If I could just keep on writing forever...

But I know that I cannot do that. He would not want that. He would thank me for remembering him and recording his story, but he would remind me that there was a lot more that needed to be done. He would tell me to finish the story, put my pen down, and get to work.

Realizing that once again he is right, I know that there is only one way that this book can end that lets me get up from this chair and breathe and move on to the next thing.

The only way that this book can end is if the story doesn't. You and I, we have to agree that the story doesn't end here. We have to agree that his life consisted of more than a few hundred pages in a book. We have to agree that our lives mean more than that. We have to agree that after I put down my pen and you put down this book, that the story doesn't end there. We have to believe that compassion can win out over hate. We have to believe that peace can conquer violence. We have to take action not out of rage or anger, not even of the righteous kind, and agree that we deserve to live in a world where empathy overpowers fear.

Can we do that? Can we agree that the story won't end here? We have to. Because the book is over. I am trusting you that his story isn't. I am putting my pen down now.

The rest is up to you.

No Tail Quotes

No Tail and I talked a lot. Constantly. He always seemed to have thoughts or insights into whatever the topic of conversation might be. Our early morning discussions in particular could go on for hours.

Sometimes, when I was struggling to understand a concept that he was trying to explain to me, he would sum up a complex idea in a single quote that was easier for me to think about and digest. I began sharing some of those quotes with people on social media.

It was one of the things that drew people into No Tail's story in the first place. They loved his unique take on life, and the quotes that he shared. When he passed away, many people reached out to me to ask if I would continue to share them now that he was gone.

Fortunately, I had written down many of our conversations before he left. I have a book with over three hundred of his quotes and observations. I have included several of my favorites here. I hope you find them as helpful as I have.

"Compassion often requires us to be willing to lift others upward toward a light that we ourselves might never see."–NT

"You are not a large enough vessel to contain all of your sorrow. You must find something to pour your sorrow into or you will drown."–NT

"A positive attitude may help you get through dark times but in order to help others, you have to be willing to strike a spark."–NT

"Hopelessness brings with it a degree of comfort. If there is no hope, there is no need to act. Nothing is expected of us. The end is inevitable. Hope, however, brings with it a degree of responsibility. Hope requires us to act."–NT

"If you would know someone's heart, examine their friends."–NT

"Strive to make the good so beautiful that evil loses its appeal."–NT

"Hope is what makes the impossible, possible."–NT

"We are never more certain of our answers than when we know we will never be put to the question."–NT

"Some people say that you are the only one that can make yourself feel inferior. I understand their point, but it is important to realize that we weren't born hating ourselves. We weren't born thinking that we were less than what we are. You may be the only that can make yourself feel inferior, but you had to be taught to do it."–NT

"The gods we choose to worship determine the demons we come to fear."–NT

"When you are lost, help someone else find their way. Maybe that was your destination all along."–NT

"A cloud does not need a silver lining to be beautiful."–NT

"Random is often the word we use when we lack the ability, or the willingness, to see the underlying cause."–NT

"If you don't feed your body, you die. If you don't feed your soul, you die as well. It's just not as obvious."–NT

"Attempt nothing and you will fail at nothing, except making a difference."–NT

prime

"Regardless of what the motivational posters say, you can't simply "choose" not to fail. You can, however, choose not to give up."–NT

"The past can be as effective a burial as a grave. Fixating on past mistakes makes you a zombie. Animated, but not truly alive."–NT

"When faced with a starving child, we should all act as though we were atheists. In that moment, if our actions are influenced by a belief in a god, or cosmic purpose, or in some divine unknown, we could be inclined to put the responsibility of feeding the child off onto a divinity or onto the universe itself. We might even callously excuse ourselves from any action at all with the argument that the child's suffering is part of some divine plan.

But in that moment, if we remove all beliefs and ideologies and we face that child only as ourselves, then we are forced to accept that we alone have the ability, and therefore the responsibility, to feed the child. In that moment, it must become only you and only them. Everything else must fade away. For just that moment, the universe contains only you and the starving child. And if you fail to act, your beliefs were irrelevant anyway."–NT

"Your actions should be guided by the lessons you've learned, not the lessons you're trying to teach someone else."–NT

"Closing your eyes does not change your reality."–NT

"Do not withhold bread from someone who is hungry, simply because they are not starving."–NT

"Humor without consent is mockery."–NT

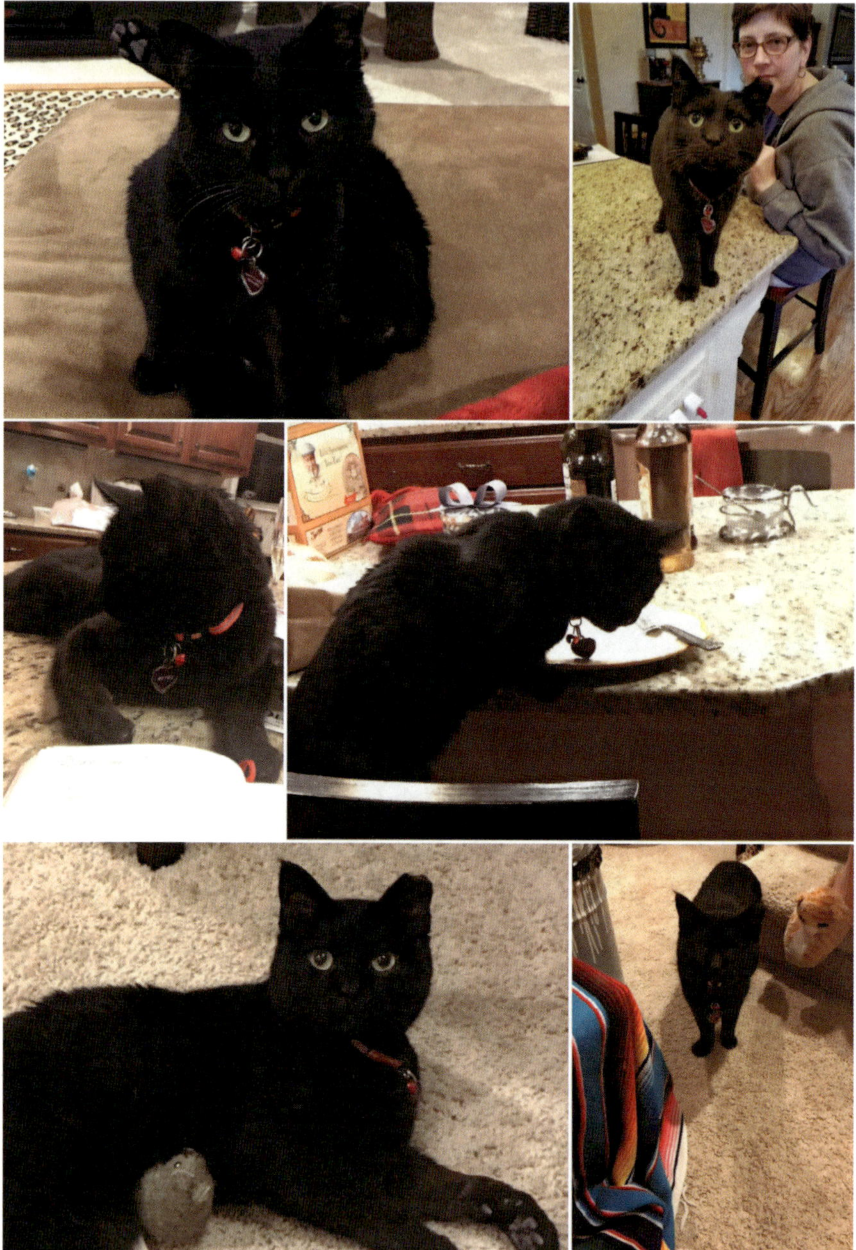

"Broadening your mind and your heart are both important, but of the two, the heart is more vital. A skilled mind can be impressive in the same way that a stage magician is impressive, but a skilled heart is real magic."–NT

"The actions of another should not create expectations of the self." – NT

"Sometimes we must attempt the impossible in order to endure the probable."–NT

"Those who speak with a casual fondness for winter because the cold helps them appreciate the warmth of spring even more, have likely never lived outside." – NT

"If you still look like the person who began the journey, then your journey isn't over." – NT

"Nostalgia is a place of rest, not a place of action. Nostalgia looks to the past. Action looks forward."–NT

"You are not obligated to fight evil, or stand against tyranny, but you ARE obligated to accept the consequences of your inaction."–NT

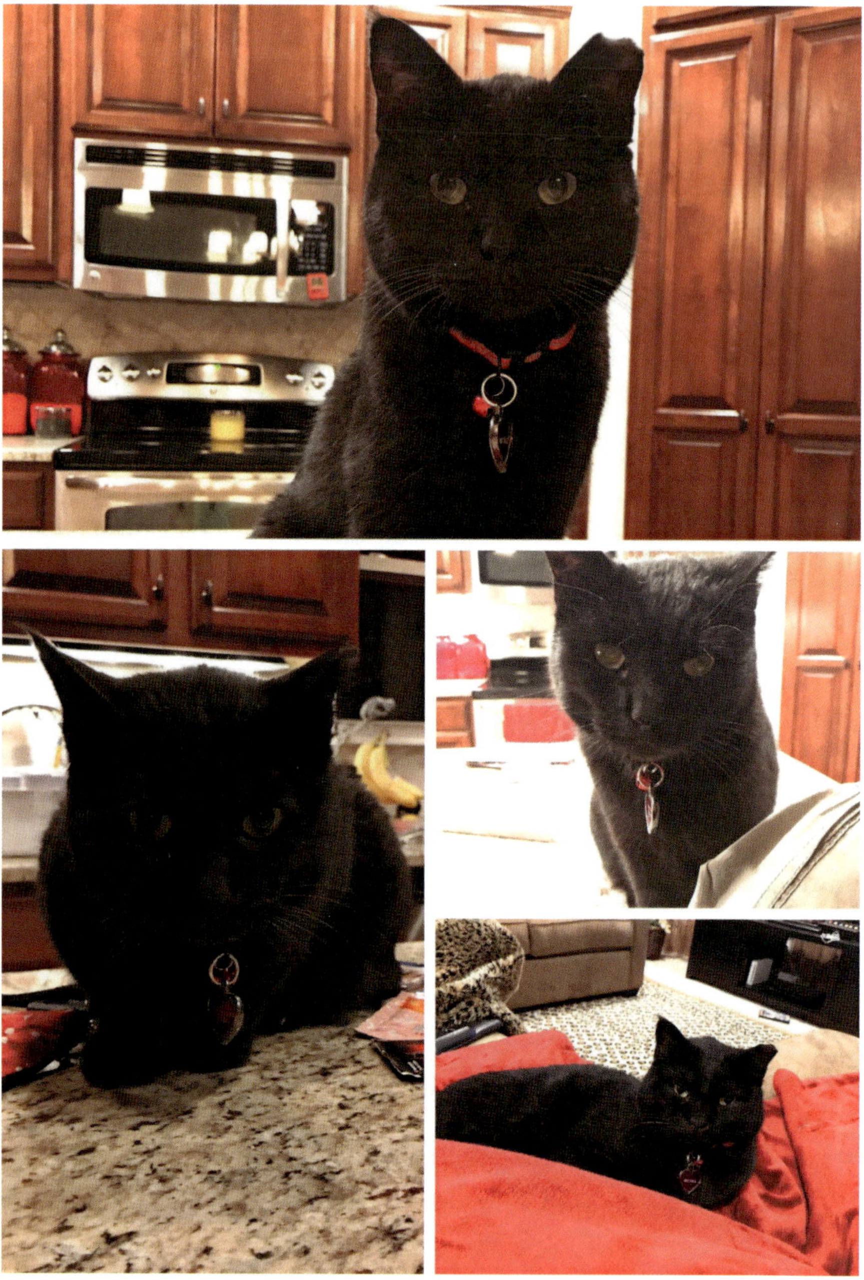

"Loud people demand that you define them by the things that they fight for. They hope that their volume will distract you from defining them by the things that they ignore."–NT

"Sometimes we are afraid to be alone because we are unsure of what else there might be around us. Sometimes though, we fear to be alone because it is ourselves that frighten us."–NT

"May we always strive to let our suffering grow compassion and not callouses."–NT

"We all have the time that we have been given. There is no free time or spare time. No one walks down the street and finds an extra hour that someone else has dropped. No one can dig through their pockets at the end of the day to gather up loose seconds. Do not let the coins of your life slip carelessly through your fingers."–NT

"One of the most powerful and truthful things a person can ever say is, "It was my fault."–NT

"Opportunity knocks but once" is an expression that originated in well-lit neighborhoods. Many people live in neighborhoods where the only knock on the door is from bill-collectors and process servers. Opportunity is never going to set foot on their street. If that is you, then you have to be the one to do the knocking. You have to go to Opportunity's door and knock, and if Opportunity doesn't answer, then you have to be willing to kick the door in."–NT

"We never make the same mistake twice. The first time we do it, it is a mistake. The second time we do it, it is a choice."–NT

"You don't sharpen steel on something soft. It is the hardness that we endure that gives us our edge."–NT

"Demons do not dwell in the darkness beneath us. They dwell in the darkness within us. Therefore, it is not a light from above, but a light from within that will save us."–NT

"Don't define yourself by what you have lost." – NT

"When you get to the point where everyone else would quit, remember, you're not everyone else."–NT

"The shackles that bind us must have something to hold onto. If we lose ourselves in search of a greater purpose, those shackles may still exist, but they will have nothing left to chain down."–NT

"Dreams without action remain nothing more than dreams, but sometimes holding onto those dreams is what helps us survive until we have the strength to act."–NT

"Healing may be the ultimate goal, but when you are hurting sometimes it is okay not to focus on the healing. Sometimes it is okay just to bleed."–NT

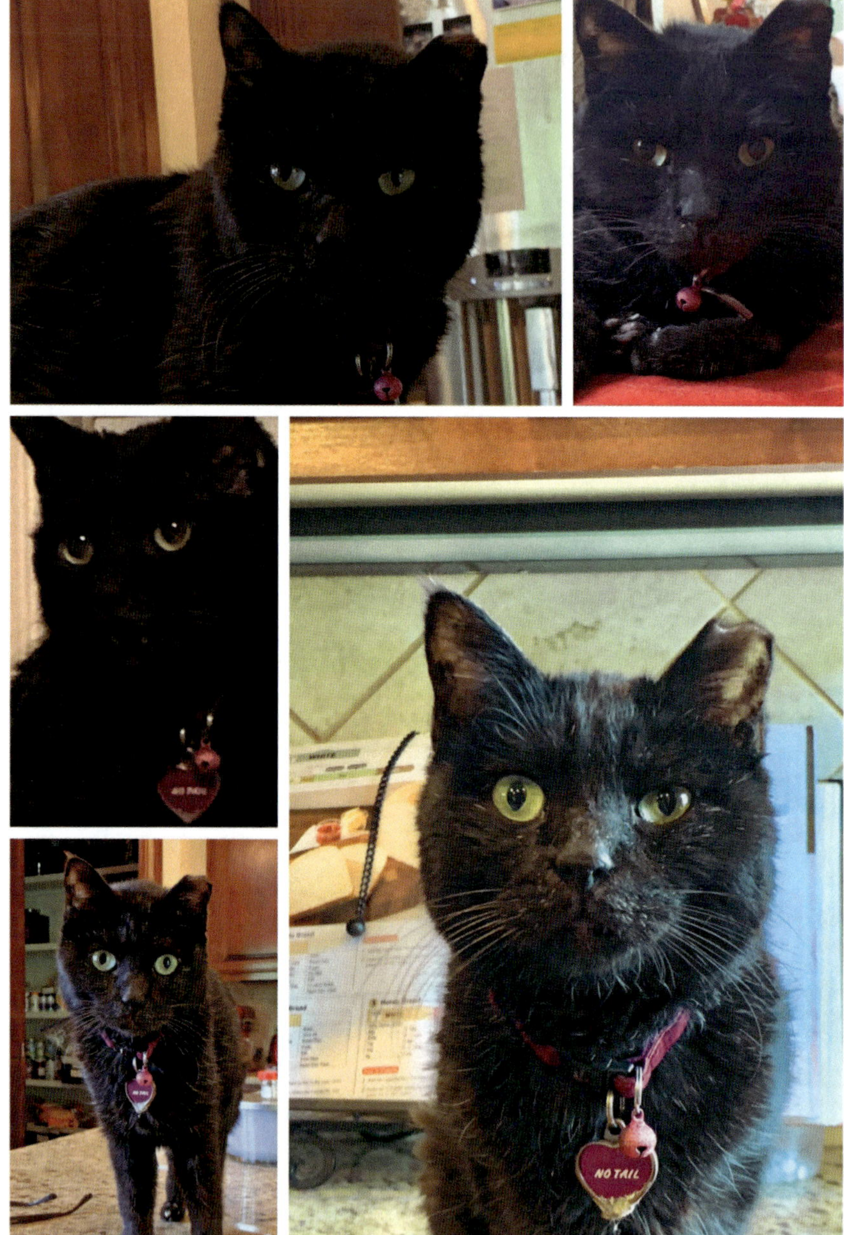
NO TAIL

"A spirit of love cannot exist without a spirit of forgiveness. We cannot love people but be unwilling to forgive them. More importantly, we cannot love ourselves until we are willing to forgive ourselves."–NT

"It is a tragedy when we believe ourselves to be the main character in someone else's story, but even more tragic when we believe ourselves to be the supporting character in our own story."–NT

"Just because the pot is the one calling the kettle black does not invalidate the fact that the kettle is black. Too often people dismiss a statement because of the source, but if the statement is true, the source does not negate the claim."–NT

"Compassion that is exclusionary is not compassion. At best it is a tool, and at worst, a weapon."–NT

"Those in power fear the one who is willing to fail."–NT

"You can't create a new tomorrow based on things you do tomorrow."–NT

"We are our own villains, but we are also our own heroes."–NT

He Is A Mountain

He is a mountain
Made too-soon old.
The full curves that separated
Abdomen from thigh,
The swells of muscle and sinew
Have eroded into deep valleys,
But still, he remains a mountain.
Seasons of storm
Upon season, upon season
Have weathered his spine,
Turning majestic peaks
Into a ragged ridge line
Of sharpened spires,
But still, he remains a mountain.
The full, fertile flesh
Has worn away,
Leaving uncushioned, ribbed slopes,
But beneath is still stone.
Beneath is still hard.
Beneath is still might.
None would look at him and say,
"Here is not a mountain."
The winter of age
Has drifted him with snow,
But his eyes still burn,
A flaming, crashing core

That brings forth mountains
In tectonic birth.
Thrusting upward
Through cataclysmic collisions
Fire and trauma
Have let him dance with the clouds,
And though he is weathered
And worn
And too-soon old
Still, he is a mountain.

—Thad Krasnesky, Dec 2023
(Written for No Tail, one month before his passing.)

Krasnesky
Manor
for Wayward Cats

Love's Calendar Is Not Our Own

Love's calendar is not our own.
The pages of its days do not turn at our hand.
We cannot hasten or postpone,
Or erase the circled dates that it has planned.
"Not yet," we say, and shake our head,
And wave our well-marked appointment book in Love's face.
"I have sorrow today instead,
And grief penciled in next week. There is no space."
Yet as we look, we see Love's pen
Has inked the word, "Now" in our itinerary,
Curtailing our solitary yen
With a timetable that's incendiary.
We jab our pen down on the page
And scrub with weeping ink at this calendar scar.
"I'm not ready," we weakly rage,
And Love embraces us as we weep and says, "You are."

—Thad Krasnesky, January, 2024, written for Nicholas Pyewacket,
who joined The Manor three weeks after No Tail passed away

The Krasnesky Manor for Wayward Cats

The Manor is a place for cats,
Raccoons, and fish, and even rats.
The dispossessed, the feral stray,
For those who've simply lost their way.
The Manor does not judge a guest
Or value one more than the rest.
It's message is, "We all have worth"
No matter what our place at birth.
We hope that all our friends will find
The Manor is a state of mind.
A welcoming place, with a friendly view,
Because many of us are Wayward Cats too.

—Thad Krasnesky, February 2022, written for The Manor,
shortly after we moved in and began to discover
the magic that still exists in some places.

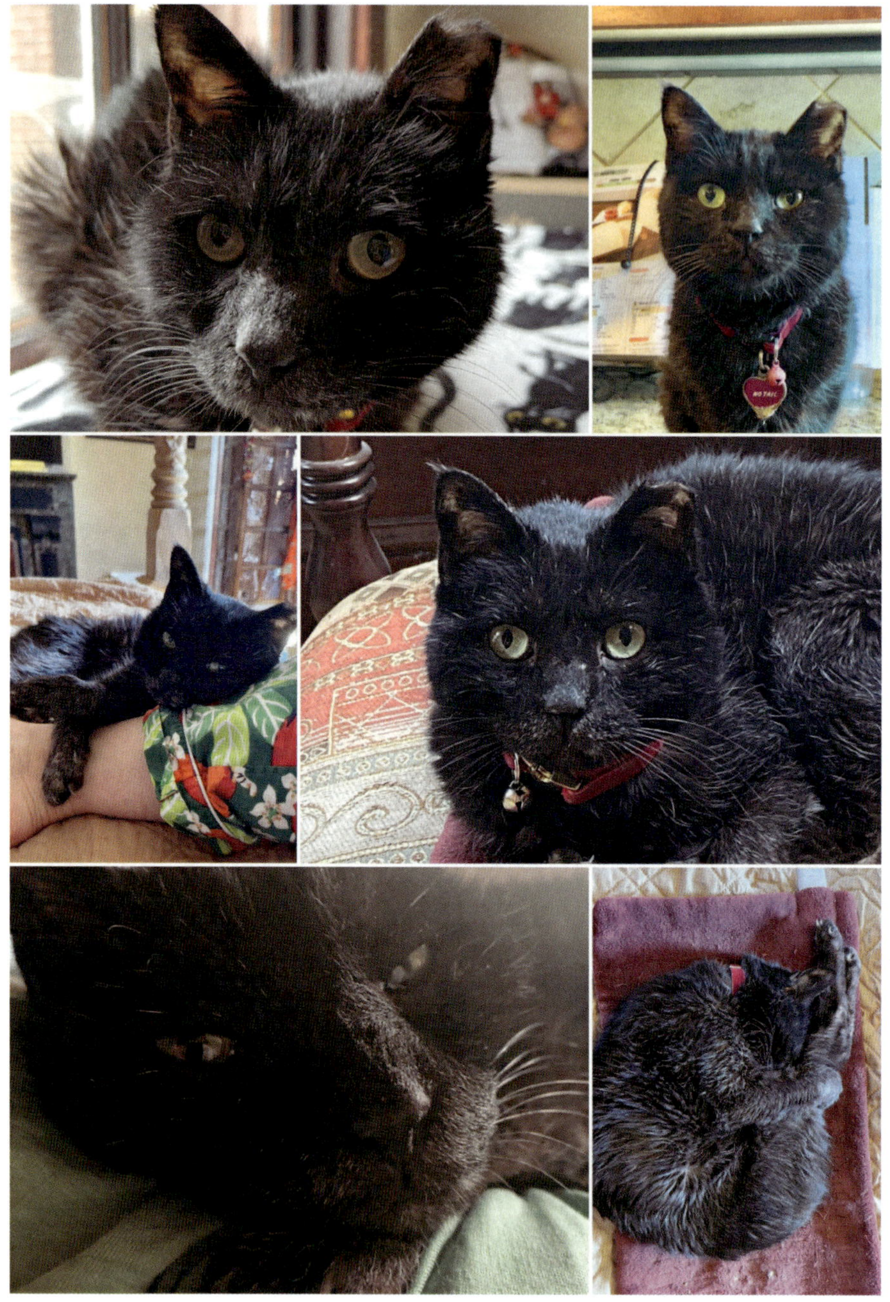

Afterword

This book was originally intended to be around 40,000 words long. It was meant to be a response to the public demand for the story of No Tail's life. At first, I wondered if I would find more than 20,000 words of story to tell. In the end, it began to creep up toward epic fantasy novel length, quickly surpassing 90,000 words, with still no end in sight.

For the sake of the concerns and attention span of others, as well as for my own sanity, I eventually pared it down to its current length, which is just over 75,000 words. There is still so much more story to tell.

For those that want to learn more about No Tail, The Krasnesky Manor for Wayward Cats, the history of The Manor, or the rest of the animals that call The Manor home, feel free to google us or check us out on social media.

There is so much more that needs to be done. It is going to take $4.1 million dollars to complete the restoration work on The Manor, and at least that much more for us to begin to fulfill the dream that we started three years ago, so please share our story, and if you have a few million friends, tell them to buy a copy of this book, or if you have a friend in Hollywood, maybe mention to them that you think this would make a great movie.

All proceeds from this book will go toward the restoration of The Manor, and the restoration of the animals and the people that come through our doors.